MW01493287

Phonics and Word Recognition Quick Checks

Table of Contents

Table of Contents

Table of Contents

Introduction

Program Overview

The *Benchmark Advance* program has ten units per grade in Grades K–6. There are ten knowledge strands on which the program revolves. Each three-week unit focuses on a Unit Topic and an Essential Question, which both relate back to the overall knowledge strand. Throughout the school year, students engage with texts in whole- and small-group settings, developing their phonics skills and applying the new strategies in context.

These Phonics and Word Recognition assessments are designed to help you evaluate your students' awareness of phonics concepts, and to provide a tool for determining when it is appropriate to use intervention materials. Below is a summary of the key *Benchmark Advance* resources used in the intervention cycle.

Teacher's Resource System and Student Reading Materials

The Teacher's Resource System and associated student readings serve as the core of the *Benchmark Advance* program. This material supports day-to-day instruction throughout the school year.

Foundational Skills Screeners

Foundational Skills Screeners consists of quick tests focused on foundational reading skills, including recognizing root words, identifying affixes, and recognizing sound patterns. *Foundational Skills Screeners* provides an efficient way to assess the general understanding of the class. Based on students' scores, you can shape instruction to meet developing areas of need before students fall behind.

Quick Checks to Intervention

The five Quick Checks books consist of short skill-based assessments designed to help you evaluate student command in key skill and knowledge areas. You may use students' performance on the Quick Checks to inform your decision of when to implement intervention. The Resource Map at the beginning of every Quick Checks book leads you to the intervention lesson(s) that focus on the skill(s) assessed in each Quick Check test.

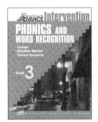 

Benchmark Advance Intervention:
Phonics and Word Recognition

The grade-specific, skill-based lessons in each Intervention book provide you with instruction and practice needed to raise struggling students to on-level proficiency. Designed to integrate with Quick Checks, these intervention resources enable you to pinpoint trouble areas and support students as they build the skill set they need for complete understanding.

Description of the Assessments

Phonics and word recognition involves sound-print correspondence: making the connection between the sounds we hear and the letters on the page. The assessments in this book evaluate students on a number of phonics skills, including recognizing consonant and vowel sounds, distinguishing homophones and homographs, and using prefixes, suffixes, and roots to make sense of words.

Each assessment focuses on a single skill and is intended for individual, one-on-one administration. There are two assessment pages per skill. The focus of each Quick Check can be found on the header of the page. You may make a copy of the test for each student you plan to assess.

Skills in this book are generally presented in sequence, mimicking the order in the day-to-day instruction of the Teacher's Resource System. However, students may be assessed on a given skill at any time, based on what is happening in the classroom or the particular needs of the student.

Every assessment may be used more than once, if needed. In most cases, the second assessment page tests different aspects of the skill or uses a different approach. In some assessments, you may note one or two items that do not test the skill listed at the top of the page. For example, in an assessment on Short Vowel *a*, you may see an item testing Long Vowel *a*. This ensures that the student being assessed is responding based on knowledge, not memory or repetition.

Teacher Administration and Answers

After you hand the Quick Check to the student, prompt the student to read the directions at the top of the page. When the student completes the assessment, collect the test and use the Answer Key in the back of this book to determine correct and incorrect answers. Place a check mark next to correct answers and an X beside incorrect answers. Add the total number of correct answers to determine the student's score. Each Quick Check has a score box for recording the student's results.

Quick Check to Phonics and Word Recognition Intervention

The score on each Quick Check may be used for record keeping or grading, but the final score on each page is less important than how the student responds along the way. Ultimately, these Quick Checks are intended as formative assessments to help you monitor students' progress and adapt instruction to individual needs.

Considering responses from the class as a whole helps determine when to move on to new or more difficult tasks. Carefully observe each student's phonics proficiency and use of word recognition skills, documenting both lessons taught and skills mastered.

Using Quick Checks to Help Guide Intervention Decisions

Based on your student's score, you may decide to offer the student resources in the *Benchmark Advance* intervention kit. The Resource Map that follows this introduction aligns the skills being assessed to the Phonics and Word Recognition Intervention lessons.

If the student scores...	Then...
between 80% and 100%	Move on to the next Quick Check or skill.
between 66% and 80%	Consider administering the Quick Check again. Continue monitoring the student during future Quick Checks.
below 66%	Use intervention resources shown in the Resource Map to provide the student with opportunities to remediate skills.

Quick Check to Intervention Resource Map

Skill	Quick Check	*Benchmark Advance* PWR Intervention Lesson	Intervention Lesson Page Number
Consonants *c* and *g*	1 (p. 2) 2 (p. 3)	**Grade 3** Lesson 16: Identify and Name Soft *g, c*	32
Silent Letters *kn, wr, gh, gn, wh*	3 (p. 4) 4 (p. 5)	**Grade 3** Lesson 69: Identify and Name Silent Letters *wr, kn, gn*	138
Short Vowel *a*	5 (p. 6) 6 (p. 7)	**Grade 3** Lesson 101: Initial Short Vowel *a*	202
Short Vowel *i*	7 (p. 8) 8 (p. 9)	**Grade 3** Lesson 102: Initial Short Vowel *i*	204
Short Vowel *o*	9 (p. 10) 10 (p. 11)	**Grade 3** Lesson 103: Initial Short Vowel *o*	206
Short Vowel *e*	11 (p. 12) 12 (p. 13)	**Grade 3** Lesson 105: Initial Short Vowel *e*	210
Short Vowel *u*	13 (p. 14) 14 (p. 15)	**Grade 3** Lesson 104: Initial Short Vowel *u*	208
Long Vowel *a*	15 (p. 16) 16 (p. 17)	**Grade 3** Lesson 1: Recognize Long Vowel Teams and Single Letters with the Sound /ā/	2
Long Vowel *i*	17 (p. 18) 18 (p. 19)	**Grade 3** Lesson 5: Recognize Lesson Recognize Long Vowel Teams and Single Letters with the Sound /ī/	10
Long Vowel *o*	19 (p. 20) 20 (p. 21)	**Grade 3** Lesson 2: Recognize Long Vowel Teams and Single Letters with the Sound /ō/	4
Long Vowel *e*	21 (p. 22) 22 (p. 23)	**Grade 3** Lesson 4: Recognize Long Vowel Teams and Single Letters with the Sound /ē/	8
r-Controlled Vowels: /är/	23 (p. 24) 24 (p. 25)	**Grade 3** Lesson 6: Identify and Name Variant Vowel /är/	12
r-Controlled Vowels: /ôr/ (or, oar, ore)	25 (p. 26) 26 (p. 27)	**Grade 3** Lesson 15: Identify and Name Variant Vowel /ôr/	30
r-Controlled Vowels: /ûr/ (er, ir, ur)	27 (p. 28) 28 (p. 29)	**Grade 3** Lesson 7: Identify and Name Variant Vowel /ûr/	14

Skill	Quick Check	*Benchmark Advance* PWR Intervention Lesson	Intervention Lesson Page Number
r-Controlled Vowels: /ir/ (*ear, eer, ere*)	29 (p. 30) 30 (p. 31)	**Grade 3** Lesson 34: Recognize *r*-Controlled Syllable Patterns with Long *e*	68
		Grades 4–6 Lesson 8: Recognize *r*-Controlled Syllable Patterns with Long *Ee*	16
r-Controlled Vowels: /ar/ (*air, are*)	31 (p. 32) 32 (p. 33)	**Grade 3** Lesson 35: Recognize *r*-Controlled Syllable Patterns with Long *a*	70
		Grades 4–6 Lesson 9: Recognize *r*-Controlled Syllable Patterns with Long *a*	18
r-Controlled Vowels: /ar/ (*ear, ere*)	33 (p. 34) 34 (p. 35)	**Grade 3** Lesson 34: Recognize *r*-Controlled Syllable Patterns with Long *e*	68
		Grades 4–6 Lesson 8: Recognize *r*-Controlled Syllable Patterns with Long *Ee*	16
Vowel Diphthong /ou/ (*ou, ow*)	35 (p. 36) 36 (p. 37)	**Grade 3** Lesson 14: Identify and Name Vowel Team *ou*	28
		Grades 4–6 Lesson 5: Identify and Name Vowel Team *ou*	10
Vowel Diphthong /oi/ (*oi, oy*)	37 (p. 38) 38 (p. 39)	**Grade 3** Lesson 67: Identify and Name Vowel Team *oi*	134
		Grades 4–6 Lesson 6: Identify and Name Vowel Team *oi*	12
Vowel Teams /o͞o/ (*oo, ou, ui, oe*)	39 (p. 40) 40 (p. 41)	**Grade 3** Lesson 13: Identify and Name Vowel Teams /o͞o/ and /o͝o/	26
		Lesson 36: Recognize Vowel Teams /o͞o/ with Syllable Patterns: *oo, ui, ew*	72
		Grades 4–6 Lesson 4: Identify and Name Vowel Teams /o͞o/ and /o͝o/	8
Vowel Teams /oo/ (*oo, ou*)	41 (p. 42) 42 (p. 43)	**Grade 3** Lesson 13: Identify and Name Vowel Teams /o͞o/ and /o͝o/	26
		Lesson 14: Identify and Name Vowel Team *ou*	28
		Grades 4–6 Lesson 4: Identify and Name Vowel Teams /o͞o/ and /o͝o/	8

Quick Check to Intervention Resource Map

Skill	Quick Check	Benchmark Advance PWR Intervention Lesson	Intervention Lesson Page Number
Variant vowel /ô/ (a, al, au, aw, augh)	43 (p. 44) 44 (p. 45)	**Grade 3**: Lesson 70: Identify and Name Vowel Sounds aw, au, al, augh	140
Closed Syllable Pattern	45 (p. 46) 46 (p. 47)	**Grade 3**: Lesson 8: Closed Syllables	16
		Lesson 50: Closed Syllables	100
		Grades 4–6 Lesson 3: Closed Syllables	6
Open Syllable Pattern	47 (p. 48) 48 (p. 49)	**Grade 3** Lesson 62: Open Syllables	124
		Grades 4–6 Lesson 2: Open Syllables	4
Consonant -le Syllable Pattern	49 (p. 50) 50 (p. 51)	**Grade 3** Lesson 72: Identify and Name le Syllables	144
		Grades 4–6 Lesson 11: Identify and Name LE Syllables	22
Vowel Team Syllable Pattern	51 (p. 52) 52 (p. 53)	**Grade 3** Lesson 59: Recognize Long Vowel Teams and Single Letters with the Sound /ō/	118
		Grades 4–6 Lesson 5: Identify and Name Vowel Team ou	10
Vowel-C-e Syllable Pattern	53 (p. 54) 54 (p. 55)	**Grades 4–6** Lesson 10: Vowel-C-e Pattern	20
Vowel-r Syllable Pattern	55 (p. 56) 56 (p. 57)	**Grade 3** Lesson 64: Identify and Name Variant Vowel /ôr/	128
		Lesson 65: Identify and Name Variant Vowel /ûr/	130
Compound Words	57 (p. 58) 58 (p. 59)	See Benchmark Advance Phonological Awareness Intervention **Grade 3** Lesson 11: Blend Spoken Words Together to Make Compound Words	22
		Lesson 12: Segment Syllables in Compound Words	24
Inflectional Endings -ed, -ing	59 (p. 60) 60 (p. 61)	**Grade 3** Lesson 11: Read Verbs with Inflectional Endings: -ed, -ing	22
		Lesson 37: Inflectional Endings with Spelling Changes	74
Irregular Plurals	61 (p. 62) 62 (p. 63)	**Grade 3** Lesson 12: Plural Nouns	24
		Lesson 39: Irregular Plural Nouns	78
		Grades 4–6 Lesson 1: Irregular Plural Nouns	2

Skill	Quick Check	*Benchmark Advance* PWR Intervention Lesson	Intervention Lesson Page Number
Prefixes: *dis-, un-*	63 (p. 64) 64 (p. 65)	**Grade 3** Lesson 20: Decode Words with Common Prefixes: *de-, dis-*	40
		Grades 4–6 Lesson 15: Decode Words with Common Prefixes: *un-*	30
		Lesson 19: Decode Words with Common Prefixes: *dis-*	38
Prefixes: *pre-, re-*	65 (p. 66) 66 (p. 67)	**Grade 3** Lesson 22: Decode Words with Common Prefixes: *re-*	44
		Grades 4–6 Lesson 14: Decode Words with Common Prefixes: *re-*	28
Prefixes: *trans-, pro-, sub-, super-, inter-*	67 (p. 68) 68 (p. 69)	**Grade 3** Lesson 24: Decode Words with Common Prefixes: *trans-, inter-*	48
		Grades 4–6 Lesson 21: Decode Words with Common Prefixes: *trans-, inter-*	42
Negative Prefixes: *de-, un-, in-, im-, dis-*	69 (p. 70) 70 (p. 71)	**Grade 3** Lesson 19 Decode Words with Common Prefixes: *un-*	38
		Grades 4–6 Lesson 15: Decode Words with Common Prefixes: *un-*	30
		Lesson 19: Decode Words with Common Prefixes: *de-, dis-*	38
Negation Prefixes: *il-, im-, in-, dis-, ir-, mis-, un-*	71 (p. 72) 72 (p. 73)	**Grade 3** Lesson 23: Decode Words with Common Prefixes: *mis-*	46
		Grades 4–6 Lesson 20: Decode Words with Common Prefixes: *mis-*	40
Prefixes That Describe Where: *pro-, em-, en-, per-, im-*	73 (p. 74) 74 (p. 75)	**Grades 4–6** Lesson 25: Decode Words with Common Prefixes: *im-*	50
Prefixes: *trans-, per-, auto-, dec-*	75 (p. 76) 76 (p. 77)	**Grades 3** Lesson 24: Decode Words with Common Prefixes: *trans-*	48
		Grades 4–6 Lesson 21: Decode Words with Common Prefixes: *trans-*	42
Prefixes: Numbers: *bi-, tri-, cent-;* Where: *inter-, em-, ex-*	77 (p. 78) 78 (p. 79)	**Grades 3** Lesson 24: Decode Words with Common Prefixes: *inter-*	48
		Grades 4–6 Lesson 21: Decode Words with Common Prefixes: *inter-*	42

Quick Check to Intervention Resource Map

Skill	Quick Check	*Benchmark Advance* PWR Intervention Lesson	Intervention Lesson Page Number
Suffixes: -er, -or	79 (p. 80) 80 (p. 81)	**Grade 3** Lesson 9: Suffixes: -er	18
		Grades 4–6 Lesson 12: Suffixes: -er	24
Suffixes: -able, -ful, -less	81 (p. 82) 82 (p. 83)	**Grade 3** Lesson 18: Suffixes: -ful, -less	36
		Grades 4–6 Lesson 16: Decode Words with Common Suffixes: -ful, -less	32
Suffixes: -ment, -ness	83 (p. 84) 84 (p. 85)	**Grade 3** Lesson 25: Decode Words with Common Suffixes: -ment	50
		Grades 4–6 Lesson 22: Decode Words with Common Suffixes: -ment	44
Adverb Suffixes: -ly, -ily, -ways, -wise	85 (p. 86) 86 (p. 87)	**Grade 3** Lesson 38: Decode Words with Common Suffixes: -ly	76
		Grades 4–6 Lesson 18: Decode Words with Common Suffixes: -ways	36
Adjective Suffixes: -ful, -ous, -ible, -able, -some	87 (p. 88) 88 (p. 89)	**Grade 3** Lesson 21: Decode Words with Common Suffixes: -able, -ible Lesson 26: Decode Words with Common Suffixes: -ous	42 52
		Grades 4–6 Lesson 26: Decode Words with Common Suffixes: -able, -ible Lesson 28: Decode Words with Common Suffixes: -ous	52 56
Adjective Suffixes: -ous, -ive, -able, -ial, -al, -less	89 (p. 90) 90 (p. 91)	**Grade 3** Lesson 21: Decode Words with Common Suffixes: -able, -al, -ial	42
		Grades 4–6 Lesson 26: Decode Words with Common Suffixes: -able, -ible	52
Adjective Suffixes: -y, -ent, -ive, -ic, -ful	91 (p. 92) 92 (p. 93)	**Grade 3** Lesson 27: Decode Words with Common Suffixes: -ive	54
		Grades 4–6 Lesson 27: Decode Words with Common Suffixes: -ent Lesson 29: Decode Words with Common Suffixes: -ive	54 58
Noun Suffixes: -dom, -ity, -tion, -ment, -ness, -ism	93 (p. 94) 94 (p. 95)	**Grade 3** Lesson 25: Decode Words with Common Suffixes: -ment, -tion	50
		Grades 4–6 Lesson 22: Decode Words with Suffixes: -ment, -tion	44
Noun Suffixes: -ology, -ant, -er, -ist, -or, -ery	95 (p. 96) 96 (p. 97)	**Grade 3**: Lesson 28: Decode Words with Suffixes: -ology Lesson 30: Decode Words with Suffixes: -ist	56 60
		Grades 4–6 Lesson 30: Suffixes: -ology Lesson 32: Decode Words with Suffixes: -ist	60 64

Skill	Quick Check	*Benchmark Advance* **PWR Intervention Lesson**	Intervention Lesson Page Number
Noun Suffixes: *-tion, -ty, -sion, -ness, -ment*	97 (p. 98) 98 (p. 99)	**Grade 3** Lesson 25: Common Suffixes: *-ment, -tion*	50
		Grades 4–6 Lesson 22: Common Suffixes: *-ment, -tion*	44
Greek and Latin Roots: *geo-, archae-, rupt, -ology*	99 (p. 100) 100 (p. 101)	**Grade 3** Lesson 28: Decode Words with Common Suffixes: *-ology*	56
		Grades 4–6 Lesson 30: Decode Words with Common Suffixes: *-ology*	60
Greek and Latin Roots: *mis, agri, duc, duct, man*	101 (p. 102) 102 (p. 103)	**Grade 3** Lesson 23: Decode Words with Common Prefixes: *mis-*	46
		Grades 4–6 Lesson 20: Decode Words with Common Prefixes: *mis-*	40
Greek and Latin Roots: *ven, migr, graph, mit*	103 (p. 104) 104 (p. 105)	**Grade 3** Lesson 28: Decode Words with Common Suffixes: *-graphy*	56
		Grades 4–6 Lesson 30: Decode Words with Common Suffixes: *-graphy*	60
Greek and Latin Roots: *spec, liter, vent, struct, aud, graphy*	105 (p. 106) 106 (p. 107)	**Grade 3** Lesson 28: Decode Words with Common Suffixes: *-graphy*	56
		Grades 4–6 Lesson 30: Decode Words with Common Suffixes: *-graphy*	60
Greek and Latin Roots: *aud, vis, form, cede, graphic*	107 (p. 108) 108 (p. 109)	**Grade 3** Lesson 28: Decode Words with Common Suffixes: *-graphic*	56
		Grades 4–6 Lesson 30: Decode Words with Common Suffixes: *-graphic*	60
Greek and Latin Science Roots: *mech, cline, mot, ang, struct, scope*	109 (p. 110) 110 (p. 111)	**Grade 3** Lesson 29: Decode Words with Common Suffixes: *-scope*	58
		Grades 4–6 Lesson 31: Decode Words with Common Suffixes: *-scope*	62
Greek Science Roots: *bio, hydro, atmo, photo, phobia*	111 (p. 112) 112 (p. 113)	**Grade 3** Lesson 29: Decode Words with Common Suffixes: *-phobia*	58
		Grades 4–6 Lesson 31: Decode Words with Common Suffixes: *-phobia*	62
Greek and Latin Roots: *aqua, amphi, fac, grat, luna, anti*	113 (p. 114) 114 (p. 115)	**Grades 4–6** Lesson 23: Decode Words with Common Prefixes: *anti-*	46
Words from Latin: *sur, sub, inter, dorm, vis*	115 (p. 116) 116 (p. 117)	**Grade 3** Lesson 24: Decode Words with Common Prefixes: *inter-*	48
		Grades 4–6 Lesson 21: Decode Words with Common Prefixes: *inter-*	42
		Lesson 24: Decode Words with Common Prefixes: *sub-*	48

Name _____ Date _____

Directions: Read the bold word. Circle the word in the row that has the same sound as the underlined letter of the bold word.

<u>c</u>ent	king	sing	wing	ring
<u>g</u>ate	jam	came	Sam	game
<u>k</u>eep	cane	pane	sane	lane
<u>g</u>em	guest	west	jest	pest
<u>c</u>amp	chat	cite	jot	kite
ba<u>s</u>e	rice	rake	ripe	rate
fla<u>g</u>	jump	shrug	ledge	flock
<u>g</u>iant	grade	shade	jade	fade

_____/8

Name _____ Date _____

Directions: Read each sentence and the four bold words below the sentence. Circle the word that best fits in the blank to complete the sentence.

1. He opened the book and read the first _____.

   pace   **page**   **pane**   **pale**

2. Please _____ me as soon as you can.

   shall   **fall**   **hall**   **call**

3. That door has a broken _____.

   hinge   **high**   **hint**   **hiss**

4. Rana just got _____ on her teeth.

   brakes   **braces**   **braves**   **brags**

5. On December 3, the weather was really _____.

   cold   **sold**   **fold**   **gold**

6. I have not seen Mallory _____ last week.

   sing   **sink**   **sing**   **since**

7. My uncle _____ me tickets to the concert.

   cold   **sold**   **fold**   **gold**

8. Jammal writes a _____ about his travels in South America.

   blow   **block**   **blog**   **blot**

____/8

Name _____ Date _____

Directions: Read the bold word. Circle the word in the row that has the same sound as the underlined letter of the bold word.

na̲me	life	wife	knife	rife
r̲ound	wing	wring	swing	fling
h̲ope	pole	sole	dole	whole
g̲naw	goat	note	moat	wrote
w̲reath	hoot	boot	shoot	root
ni̲ght	beak	beg	beat	Beth
k̲nee	noose	goose	loose	choose
wh̲o	rim	brim	whim	dim

___/8

Grades 3–6 • Benchmark Advance • **Phonics and Word Recognition** Quick Checks • © Benchmark Education Company, LLC

Name _____ Date _____

Directions: Read each sentence and the four bold words below the sentence. Circle the word that best fits in the blank to complete the sentence.

1. Shamika will _____ the answer to that question.

   glow　　　**flow**　　　**know**　　　**crow**

2. He will use newspaper to _____ the box.

   trap　　　**wrap**　　　**flap**　　　**nap**

3. The _____ in Mrs. Brady's garden has a red hat.

   gnome　　　**foam**　　　**home**　　　**roam**

4. Mom added some more flour to the _____.

   dog　　　**dough**　　　**doubt**　　　**dock**

5. Did you _____ on the door?

   clock　　　**shock**　　　**block**　　　**knock**

6. I can't tell _____ jacket is on the chair.

   nose　　　**whose**　　　**rose**　　　**nose**

7. Perry broke his _____ when he fell off the ladder.

   list　　　**whist**　　　**wrist**　　　**mist**

8. The _____ on the corner said "One Way."

   sign　　　**sick**　　　**silk**　　　**sink**

____/8

Name _____ Date _____

Directions: Read the bold word. Circle the word in the row that has the same vowel sound as the bold word.

hand	cub	cog	cab	cage
last	branch	brake	brunch	broke
take	pan	pine	pen	pane
camp	block	bake	black	ball
act	fat	fate	foot	fit
age	tape	tan	tap	tall
has	lush	lash	late	lost
plant	grim	grime	gram	game

_____/8

Name _____ Date _____

Directions: Read each sentence and the four bold words below the sentence. Circle the word that best fits in the blank to complete the sentence.

1. Neil and his friends play in a _____.

   bend   **bane**   **bond**   **band**

2. Roberta got _____ when I teased her.

   mad   **made**   **may**   **mark**

3. Uncle Van keeps his tools in that old _____.

   shack   **shock**   **shawl**   **shall**

4. Kelly used a _____ to hang her picture on the wall.

   take   **talk**   **tuck**   **tack**

5. We watched a tiny _____ carry a leaf.

   ate   **on**   **ant**   **unto**

6. The man filled a _____ with potatoes.

   sack   **sake**   **sick**   **soak**

7. Everyone had a _____ time at the party.

   grade   **grind**   **ground**   **grand**

8. Grandpa used an _____ to cut down the tree.

   ex   **ox**   **ax**   **age**

_____/8

Name _____ Date _____

Directions: Read the bold word. Circle the word in the row that has the same vowel sound as the bold word.

miss	like	lack	lick	lake
ring	side	said	sit	set
bike	pin	pine	pink	pan
will	brine	brag	bran	bring
ride	mill	mile	mail	mall
inch	dim	dam	dime	dame
give	slide	sly	slid	sleep
did	chin	china	chant	chain

____/8

Name _____ Date _____

Directions: Read each sentence. Circle the word that completes each sentence correctly.

1. You can _____ an apple from the tree.

    pack   **pike**   **pick**   **puck**

2. I got a new catcher's _____ for my birthday.

    mitt   **mite**   **mutt**   **met**

3. Brenna says she _____ come over later.

    while   **well**   **wall**   **will**

4. Can we get _____ of these bags of trash?

    red   **rid**   **ride**   **rod**

5. Did your team _____ the game?

    when   **wine**   **wan**   **win**

6. We need to _____ this bag with sand.

    file   **fell**   **fill**   **fall**

7. Have you met Jerry and his _____ brother Terry?

    twin   **tine**   **twine**   **ten**

8. I need a piece of _____ to tie this package.

    strong   **strang**   **string**   **strength**

____/8

Name _____ Date _____

Directions: Read the bold word. Circle the word in the row that has the same vowel sound as the bold word.

fox	add	odd	ode	ade
rose	can	cone	con	cane
flop	get	gate	goat	got
wrong	stick	stock	stoke	stack
clock	pop	pep	pipe	pope
lone	not	note	net	nut
sob	joke	Jack	juke	jock
top	mode	mad	mod	made

____/8

Name _____ Date _____

Directions: Read each sentence and the four bold words below the sentence. Circle the word that best fits in the blank to complete the sentence.

1. Dad bought a new fishing _____.

   rode   **red**   **rod**   **rude**

2. The Fourth of July was really _____.

   hot   **hat**   **hit**   **hut**

3. They wanted to _____ because the movie ending was sad.

   song   **say**   **sap**   **sob**

4. My aunt opened a new gift _____.

   ship   **shop**   **shap**   **sheep**

5. Mr. Chase works in Boston as a traffic _____.

   cop   **cup**   **cope**   **cap**

6. Did you remember to _____ the door?

   look   **lack**   **lock**   **lake**

7. Mom is very _____ of our cousins.

   fun   **fond**   **fund**   **fan**

8. Melanie has _____ brown hair.

   lone   **lung**   **lane**   **long**

_____/8

Name _____ Date _____

Directions: Read the bold word. Circle the word in the row that has the same vowel sound as the bold word.

fell	went	we	want	why
end	beet	bat	bet	bit
me	shed	shade	said	she
get	stop	step	steep	stub
self	peep	pep	pipe	pup
rent	bell	bill	bull	ball
help	just	jeep	jump	jest
next	loft	lift	left	leaf

_____/8

Name _____ Date _____

Directions: Read each sentence and the four bold words below the sentence. Circle the word that best fits in the blank to complete the sentence.

1. Lisa wants to _____ a new bike.

    gate   **get**   **goat**   **gut**

2. If we go early, _____ we will get good seats.

    thin   **than**   **then**   **the**

3. Please _____ the table for dinner.

    set   **sat**   **seat**   **sit**

4. Jared _____ the dogs and took them for a walk.

    feed   **fad**   **fade**   **fed**

5. Aunt Belle promised to _____ me a letter.

    sand   **seen**   **send**   **sane**

6. I have never _____ your friend Henry.

    met   **meet**   **mat**   **mate**

7. Kevin _____ bowling yesterday.

    want   **win**   **went**   **wine**

8. Her phone _____ out of her backpack.

    fell   **fill**   **feel**   **full**

_____/8

Name _____ Date _____

Directions: Read the bold word. Circle the word in the row that has the same vowel sound as the bold word.

dull	mat	mitt	mute	mutt
rust	cube	cub	cab	cob
much	stone	stand	Sue	stun
hunt	check	chuck	chock	chick
bump	lug	log	luge	loge
huge	mole	mile	mull	mule
sum	fume	fuss	full	four
bug	dude	dad	dud	did

_____/8

Name _____ Date _____

Directions: Read each sentence and the four bold words below the sentence. Circle the word that best fits in the blank to complete the sentence.

1. Grandpa visited _____ for two weeks.

   as   **is**   **us**   **on**

2. The man broke off a large _____ of cheese.

   honk   **hand**   **hack**   **hunk**

3. We _____ finish our chores before we can go to the park.

   must   **mast**   **mist**   **most**

4. Darla likes to _____ every morning before school.

   rune   **ran**   **run**   **rain**

5. The squirrel grabbed a _____ and ran up the tree.

   nut   **net**   **not**   **note**

6. The next batter tried to _____ the ball toward third base.

   bone   **bent**   **ban**   **bunt**

7. Mindy _____ the apple into six pieces.

   cot   **cut**   **cute**   **coat**

8. We had to _____ water out of the basement after the storm.

   pump   **pop**   **pomp**   **pan**

____/8

Name _____ Date _____

Directions: Point to each row and read the words aloud. Circle any words in which you hear the long vowel *a* sound.

1.	jam	escape	playpen
2.	stamp	basement	landing
3.	relay	grant	painter
4.	grain	remark	gateway

_____/12

Name _____ Date _____

Directions: Point to each row and read the words aloud. Circle any words in which you hear the long vowel *a* sound.

1.	gray	race	wake
2.	replace	past	faint
3.	training	stack	afraid
4.	lazy	maybe	pan

_____/12

Name _____ Date _____

Directions: Point to each row and read the words aloud. Circle any words in which you hear the long vowel *i* sound.

1.	bride	driver	pilot
2.	silent	lint	unties
3.	flight	reply	time
4.	flipper	describe	chin

_____/12

Name _____ Date _____

Directions: Point to each row and read the words aloud. Circle any words in which you hear the long vowel *i* sound.

1.	sideline	white	swim
2.	twice	trim	highlight
3.	tonight	kind	pilot
4.	refried	pick	retry

_____/12

Name _____ Date _____

Directions: Point to each row and read the words aloud. Circle any words in which you hear the long vowel *o* sound.

1. stove	snowfall	soapstone
2. sock	below	alone
3. polo	hopeful	bowling
4. remote	prop	whole

____/12

Name _____ Date _____

Directions: Point to each row and read the words aloud. Circle any words in which you hear the long vowel *o* sound.

1. grown	lock	showman
2. throat	homeland	awoke
3. open	solo	explode
4. chop	token	coatcheck

_____/12

Name _____ Date _____

Directions: Point to each row and read the words aloud. Circle any words in which you hear the long vowel *e* sound.

1.	kettle	cheat	sweetly
2.	greet	these	valley
3.	keyhole	peanut	pencil
4.	fleece	fifteen	desk

____/12

Grades 3–6 • Benchmark Advance • **Phonics and Word Recognition** Quick Checks • © Benchmark Education Company, LLC

Name _____ Date _____

Directions: Point to each row and read the words aloud. Circle any words in which you hear the long vowel *e* sound.

1.	wheat	vest	beet
2.	leaf	street	cheese
3.	lemon	steeply	breathe
4.	pleasing	treetop	breeze

_____/12

Name _____ Date _____

Directions: Point to each row and read the words aloud. Circle any words in which you hear the *r*-controlled vowel sound /är/ as in *car*.

1. harvest	sparkle	pack
2. marble	barber	remark
3. farmer	cartoon	guitar
4. bone	garden	artist

_____/12

Name _____ Date _____

Directions: Point to each row and read the words aloud. Circle any words in which you hear the *r*-controlled vowel sound /är/ as in *car*.

1. yarn	heart	rain
2. scarlet	apartment	marble
3. float	garbage	delay
4. pardon	between	alarm

_____/12

Name _____ Date _____

Directions: Point to each row and read the words aloud. Circle any words in which you hear the *r*-controlled vowel sound /ôr/ as in *corn*.

1. afford	ignore	tire
2. report	outdoor	coral
3. core	forest	hornet
4. popcorn	explore	morning

____/12

Name _____ Date _____

Directions: Point to each row and read the words aloud. Circle any words in which you hear the *r*-controlled vowel sound /ôr/ as in *corn*.

1.	before	forget	tornado
2.	storm	alarm	orbit
3.	target	discord	department
4.	roar	library	corner

_____/12

Name _____ Date _____

Directions: Point to each row and read the words aloud. Circle any words in which you hear the *r*-controlled vowel sound /ûr/ as in *bird*.

1.	adventure	hurdle	nursery
2.	pearl	third	barge
3.	nose	murmur	picture
4.	mercy	curtain	furnace

_____/12

Grades 3–6 • Benchmark Advance • **Phonics and Word Recognition** Quick Checks • © Benchmark Education Company, LLC

Name _____ Date _____

Directions: Point to each row and read the words aloud. Circle any words in which you hear the *r*-controlled vowel sound /ûr/ as in *bird*.

1.	sherbet	curtail	thirsty
2.	purple	firm	short
3.	barn	yarn	wore
4.	occurred	sturdy	circle

_____/12

Name _____ Date _____

Directions: Point to each row and read the words aloud. Circle any words in which you hear the *r*-controlled vowel sound /ir/ as in *gear*.

1.	clear	reindeer	never
2.	career	interfere	atmosphere
3.	disappear	fare	engineer
4.	weary	revered	year

_____/12

Name _____ Date _____

Directions: Point to each word and read the word aloud. Circle any words in which you hear the *r*-controlled vowel sound /ir/ as in *gear*.

1.	earnest	dreary	cheerful
2.	appear	hire	roar
3.	there	sincere	beard
4.	volunteer	smear	pioneer

____/12

Name _____ Date _____

Directions: Point to each row and read the words aloud. Circle any words in which you hear the *r*-controlled vowel sound /ar/ as in *rare*.

1. hair	compare	software
2. square	shore	careful
3. beware	dairy	airport
4. here	glare	repair

_____/12

Name _____ Date _____

Directions: Point to each row and read the words aloud. Circle any words in which you hear the *r*-controlled vowel sound /ar/ as in *rare*.

1.	arm	were	prepare
2.	care	downstairs	share
3.	pore	flare	deer
4.	prairie	fair	declare

____/12

Name _____ Date _____

Directions: Point to each row and read the words aloud. Circle any words in which you hear the *r*-controlled vowel sound /ar/ as in *spear*.

1. sour	everywhere	therefore
2. flower	where	swear
3. somewhere	wear	bear

_____/9

Name _____ Date _____

Directions: Point to each row and read the words aloud. Circle any words in which you hear the *r*-controlled vowel sound /ar/ as in *spear*.

1. fear	shear	swear
2. steer	before	power
3. there	shower	here

_____/9

Name _____ Date _____

Directions: Point to each row and read the words aloud. Circle any words in which you hear the vowel sound /ou/ as in *crown*.

1.	crowd	house	hole
2.	down	tower	mountain
3.	done	brown	towel
4.	prowl	shower	shout

_____/12

Name _____ Date _____

Directions: Point to each row and read the words aloud. Circle any words in which you hear the vowel sound /ou/ as in *crown*.

1. proud	blouse	sound
2. tune	spout	new
3. doubt	ground	snout
4. about	load	sprout

_____/12

Name _____ Date _____

Directions: Point to each row and read the words aloud. Circle any words in which you hear the vowel sound /oi/ as in *foil*.

1.	spoil	soil	voice
2.	joint	destroy	say
3.	paint	toil	point
4.	noise	boil	annoy

_____/12

Name _____ Date _____

Directions: Point to each row and read the words aloud. Circle any words in which you hear the vowel sound /oi/ as in *foil*.

1. join	coin	royalty
2. toys	coal	joyful
3. coil	employ	choice
4. nose	moist	hoist

____/12

Name _____ Date _____

Directions: Point to each row and read the words aloud. Circle any words in which you hear the vowel team /o͞o/ as in *tool*.

1.	fool	group	juice
2.	shoe	fruit	hoop
3.	toll	troop	joke
4.	goose	you	canoe

_____/12

Name _____ Date _____

Directions: Point to each row and read the words aloud. Circle any words in which you hear the vowel team /o͞o/ as in *tool*.

1. soup	window	raccoon
2. groom	sob	stop
3. through	bloom	suit
4. hoot	loose	mousse

____/12

Name _____ Date _____

Directions: Point to each row and read the words aloud. Circle any words in which you hear the vowel team /oŏ/ as in *book*.

1.	food	could	wooden
2.	hood	look	good
3.	shock	wood	wade
4.	took	would	cook

____/12

Name _____ Date _____

Directions: Point to each row and read the words aloud. Circle any words in which you hear the vowel team /o͝o/ as in *book*.

1.	stood	should	luck
2.	shook	swoosh	goodbye
3.	rookie	woolen	brook
4.	lock	nook	understood

____/12

Name _____ Date _____

Directions: Beginning with row 1, point to each word and read the word aloud.
Next, draw a line to divide the word into syllables.

1.	because	awful	always
2.	wallet	also	withdraw
3.	author	halter	falling
4.	hauling	sausage	smaller

____/12

Grades 3–6 • Benchmark Advance • **Phonics and Word Recognition** Quick Checks • © Benchmark Education Company, LLC

Name _____ Date _____

Directions: Beginning with row 1, point to each word and read the word aloud. Next, draw a line to divide the word into syllables.

1. lawful	drawing	launchpad
2. faultless	pausing	daughter
3. drywall	crawling	hallway
4. almost	coleslaw	caution

____/12

Name _____ Date _____

Directions: Beginning with row 1, point to each word and read the word aloud. Next, draw a line to divide the word into syllables.

1.	absent	tennis	comet
2.	velvet	magnet	happen
3.	tunnel	channel	pilgrim
4.	button	fabric	cactus

_____/12

Name _____ Date _____

Directions: Beginning with row 1, point to each word and read the word aloud. Next, draw a line to divide the word into syllables.

1. contrast	trumpet	bankrupt
2. wisdom	mammal	hundred
3. blossom	publish	combat
4. splendid	congress	custom

_____/12

Name _____ Date _____

Directions: Beginning with row 1, point to each word and read the word aloud. Next, draw a line to divide the word into syllables.

1.	pilot	total	fever
2.	pony	event	zero
3.	local	minus	bacon
4.	navy	able	remind

_____/12

Grades 3–6 • Benchmark Advance • **Phonics and Word Recognition** Quick Checks • © Benchmark Education Company, LLC

Name _____ Date _____

Directions: Beginning with row 1, point to each word and read the word aloud.
Next, draw a line to divide the word into syllables.

1.	remit	cider	minor
2.	slogan	trophy	rotate
3.	meter	brutal	vacant
4.	ivy	moment	frequent

_____/12

Name _____ Date _____

Directions: Beginning with row 1, point to each word and read the word aloud. Next, draw a line to divide the word into syllables.

1.	tickle	marble	uncle
2.	settle	eagle	noble
3.	ankle	bundle	needle
4.	candle	temple	bottle

____/12

Name _____ Date _____

Directions: Beginning with row 1, point to each word and read the word aloud.
Next, draw a line to divide the word into syllables.

1. sensible	pickle	struggle
2. throttle	entitle	assemble
3. resemble	tangle	multiple
4. mumble	particle	visible

____/12

Name _____ Date _____

Directions: Beginning with row 1, point to each word and read the word aloud. Next, draw a line to divide the word into syllables.

1. ahead	deadly	soapy
2. weather	sounded	certain
3. breakfast	deadline	feather
4. squealing	peanut	tainted

_____/12

Name _____ Date _____

Directions: Beginning with row 1, point to each word and read the word aloud.
Next, draw a line to divide the word into syllables.

1.	healthy	frowning	portrait
2.	rounded	pleasure	meatball
3.	spoilage	curtain	goalie
4.	furious	clowning	jealous

____/12

Name _____ Date _____

Directions: Beginning with row 1, point to each word and read the word aloud. Next, draw a line to divide the word into syllables.

1. decline	arrive	behave
2. misspoke	propose	excite
3. repave	invite	engrave
4. remote	refute	restate

____/12

Name _____ Date _____

Directions: Beginning with row 1, point to each word and read the word aloud.
Next, draw a line to divide the word into syllables.

1.	mistake	vibrate	bespoke
2.	demote	deprive	repute
3.	mutate	impose	snowflake
4.	confine	simulate	alpine

_____/12

Name _____ Date _____

Directions: Beginning with row 1, point to each word and read the word aloud.
Next, draw a line to divide the word into syllables.

1.	curling	disturb	compare
2.	firmly	cursive	current
3.	beware	thermos	surprise
4.	verbal	porches	hermit

____/12

Name _____ Date _____

Directions: Beginning with row 1, point to each word and read the word aloud. Next, draw a line to divide the word into syllables.

1.	purchase	emerge	porcupine
2.	inspector	journal	surround
3.	versus	surrender	sirloin
4.	survival	remorse	organize

_____/12

Name _____ Date _____

Directions: Read each sentence. Circle the compound word in the sentence and write the two smaller words that make up the compound word on the line.

1. Put the dirty plates in the dishwasher.

_____

2. Mr. Hollings moved the television downstairs.

_____

3. The sunlight streamed through the window.

_____

4. Tyler is playing with his friends in the backyard.

_____

5. Fran used a flashlight while walking at night.

_____

6. Mrs. Prieto bought a new necklace.

_____

8. I plugged my headphones into the computer.

_____

9. The restaurant was across the street from the courthouse.

_____

10. Carter's teammate won the long distance race.

_____

_____/10

Grades 3–6 • Benchmark Advance • **Phonics and Word Recognition** Quick Checks • © Benchmark Education Company, LLC

Name _____ Date _____

Directions: Read each sentence and the three bold words below the sentence. Circle the word that best fits in the blank to complete the compound word.

1. We heard foot_____ coming up the stairs.

   prints   **rests**   **steps**

2. Lila went to the store with_____ her parents.

   out   **held**   **draw**

3. The dog ran _____side our car for two blocks.

   off   **along**   **down**

4. Ms. Brownell _____looked my mistake this time.

   over   **out**   **up**

5. Sarah has many toys in her bed_____.

   time   **side**   **room**

6. Dale put on his sun_____ and walked out the door.

   light   **shine**   **glasses**

7. The night_____ helps her see.

   time   **light**   **gown**

8. There is a yellow rain_____ hanging in the closet.

   coat   **bow**   **storm**

_____/8

Name _____ Date _____

Directions: Read each sentence and the three bold words below the sentence. Circle the verb with the inflectional ending *-ed* or *-ing* that best fits in the blank.

1. Ricardo _____ the vase on the table.

   placed   **placing**   **placeed**

2. The soccer player _____ the ball into the net.

   blasted   **blasting**   **blastted**

3. The boy was _____ a stack of books.

   carrieing   **carrying**   **carried**

4. I saw Bruce _____ from the car window.

   waved   **waveing**   **waving**

5. The bird _____ into the window.

   bumping   **bumped**   **bumpped**

6. The children are _____ on the ice.

   skated   **skating**   **skateing**

7. The building was _____ in six months.

   constructed   **constructted**   **constructing**

8. Mr. Jenkins _____ to Delia to step forward.

   motionned   **motioning**   **motioned**

____/8

Grades 3–6 • Benchmark Advance • **Phonics and Word Recognition** Quick Checks • © Benchmark Education Company, LLC

Name _____ Date _____

Directions: Read each sentence. Using one of the inflectional endings in the box, write the correct form of the bold word on the line to complete the sentence.

-ed	-ing

1. The art teacher _____ Ben with his painting.

   assist

2. He is _____ a sculpture made from glue and newspaper.

   create

3. Brian lost his ticket so he was _____ entry to the concert.

   deny

4. Denise was _____ after she fell on the stairs.

   limp

5. The children _____ up their rooms.

   tidy

6. Our friends _____ at the cabin.

   arrive

7. "I am _____ to his question," said Alison.

   respond

8. The chef _____ all the ingredients in a bowl.

   mix

9. The brothers were _____ over a ball.

   fight

_____/9

Name _____ Date _____

Directions: Read each sentence and the three bold words below the sentence. Circle the form of the irregular plural noun that best fits in the blank.

1. Those new _____ are in the drawer.

   knife   **knifes**   **knives**

2. The dog herded the _____.

   sheep   **sheeps**   **sheepes**

3. Beth cut the cookie into two _____.

   halfes   **halfs**   **halves**

4. You can see active _____ in Hawaii and Iceland.

   volcano   **volcanos**   **volcanoes**

5. Seven _____ were born last spring.

   calfes   **calfs**   **calves**

6. Stanton heard a pack of _____ howling.

   wolfs   **wolfes**   **wolves**

7. Our _____ were soaked after we walked home in the rain.

   footes   **foots**   **feet**

8. All of the _____ were full of books.

   shelfes   **shelfs**   **shelves**

____/8

Name _____ Date _____

Directions: Read each sentence. Write the irregular plural form of the bold singular noun in the blank to complete the sentence.

1. Fairies and _____ are characters in many myths and legends.　　　　　　　　　　　　　　　　**elf**

2. The _____ of bread were stale.　　　　　**loaf**

3. Many _____ grow in the Sonoran desert.　　　**cactus**

4. The _____ met after soccer practice.　　　　**child**

5. Lisa grew _____ in her garden.　　　　　　**tomato**

6. A herd of _____ roamed the grasslands.　　　**bison**

7. We often hear _____ when hiking in the canyon.　**echo**

8. Three _____ crossed the road.　　　　　　**deer**

9. Mashed _____ and ham is Sam's favorite meal.　**potato**

10. The horses stomped their _____.　　　　　**hoof**

_____/10

Name _____ Date _____

Directions: Read each sentence and the two bold words below the sentence.
Circle the word that best fits in the blank.

1. My mother _____ junk food of all kinds.

   dislikes   **unlikes**

2. "Junk food is so _____!" she claims.

   dishealthy   **unhealthy**

3. Sometimes, I _____ with her idea.

   disagree   **unagree**

4. At our house, chocolate chip cookies _____ quickly.

   disappear   **unappear**

5. My father is _____ to skip dessert.

   disable   **unable**

6. It is not _____ for him to have a snack in the afternoon.

   discommon   **uncommon**

7. My mother often _____ candy in my brother's pockets.

   discovers   **uncovers**

8. I am _____ about who is right!

   discertain   **uncertain**

_____/8

Grades 3–6 • Benchmark Advance • Phonics and Word Recognition Quick Checks • © Benchmark Education Company, LLC

Name _____ Date _____

Directions: Read each sentence. Write the correct prefix from the box on the line to complete the word in the sentence.

dis-	un-

1. If you _____connect my computer, I can't watch the game.

2. My favorite soccer team is _____defeated!

3. A loss tonight would be _____expected.

4. One player was _____qualified for hurting a player on the other team.

5. We should all _____approve of poor behavior on the field.

6. In many soccer games, a tie score can remain _____broken.

7. The talent on these two teams is a little _____even.

8. Who do I think will win? I'm _____decided.

9. I would be _____honest if I said I didn't care.

10. The game will be _____continued if a thunderstorm moves in.

_____/10

Name _____ Date _____

Directions: Read each sentence and the two bold words below the sentence. Circle the word that best fits in the blank.

1. Last week, I volunteered at my sister's _____.

   preschool   **reschool**

2. Mrs. Clooney had _____ some activities in the kitchen.

   preplanned   **replanned**

3. Before we began, we _____ the schedule and the recipe with her.

   previewed   **reviewed**

4. We planned to bake apples, so we _____ the oven before baking.

   preheated   **reheated**

5. We _____ the spice cabinet because we forgot the nutmeg.

   preopened   **reopened**

6. Mrs. Clooney asked us to _____ the apple cores and skins in the compost.

   precycle   **recycle**

7. I wanted to _____ Mrs. Clooney's class the very next day.

   previsit   **revisit**

8. I don't _____ ever having more fun!

   precall   **recall**

_____/8

Grades 3–6 • Benchmark Advance • **Phonics and Word Recognition** Quick Checks • © Benchmark Education Company, LLC

Name _____ Date _____

Directions: Read each sentence. Write the correct prefix from the box on the line to complete the word in the sentence.

pre-	re-

1. The _____view for the show's new season made me want to watch it.

2. The show would feature a _____union of my two favorite detectives.

3. I _____scheduled my guitar lesson so I could watch the show.

4. In the first episode, a master criminal from last season _____appeared.

5. This new season _____sented a new and exciting character.

6. A new detective who was only ten years old brought a _____freshing change.

7. This young detective helped _____cover a million dollars!

8. They _____paid him for his work by giving him a real job on the police force.

_____/8

Name _____ Date _____

Directions: Read each sentence and the three bold prefixes below the sentence. Circle the prefix that best fits in the blank to complete the word in the sentence.

1. I had never been on a _____way train before.

   trans-   **sub-**   **pro-**

2. Twice, we had to _____fer to different trains.

   super-   **inter-**   **trans-**

3. Near the bus stop, workers held a _____labor demonstration.

   sub-   **pro-**   **inter-**

4. My uncle is a _____visor for the railroad.

   pro-   **super-**   **inter-**

5. We went to a hockey game between _____city rivals.

   trans-   **super-**   **inter-**

6. All of my cousins read a player _____file.

   sub-   **trans-**   **pro-**

7. My sister had to _____late the words of the Canadian national anthem.

   inter-   **trans-**   **sub-**

8. After the first period of the game, there was a short _____mission.

   trans-   **inter-**   **super-**

____/8

Name _____ Date _____

Directions: Read each sentence. Write the correct prefix from the box on the line to complete the word in the sentence.

trans-	pro-	sub-	super-	inter-

1. Today, my cousin Rachel had her _____view to join the U.S. Navy.

2. She has always wanted to serve on the crew of a naval _____marine.

3. She likes the idea of _____porting goods around the world.

4. Everyone in our family is _____military.

5. Rachel took classes in _____personal relationships and diplomacy.

6. In my eyes, Rachel is a _____hero.

7. She has _____formed herself from a weak student to a strong athlete.

8. She is _____active at improving her speed.

9. One time, we went to the harbor to see a _____tanker unload.

10. Rachel wanted to become a _____visor of a business when she was younger.

____/10

Name _____ Date _____

Directions: Read each sentence and the three bold prefixes below the sentence. Circle the prefix that best fits in the blank to complete the word in the sentence.

1. Jon _____likes sledding and ice skating.

   dis-   **in-**   **un-**

2. He says too much exercise in the cold leaves him _____hydrated.

   un-   **im-**   **de-**

3. He says it is _____possible to stay warm.

   im-   **de-**   **un-**

4. He hates standing around in an _____heated hut.

   im-   **de-**   **un-**

5. As soon as he gets to the sledding hill, he wants to _____part.

   de-   **im-**   **in-**

6. He tries to _____crease his television hours.

   un-   **dis-**   **de-**

7. He simply _____agrees with outdoor sports lovers.

   de-   **dis-**   **in-**

8. For Jon, a day without technology seems _____complete.

   un-   **dis-**   **in-**

_____/8

Name _____ Date _____

Directions: Read each sentence. Write the correct prefix from the box on the line to complete the word in the sentence.

de-	un-	in-	im-	dis-

1. We know that people, including athletes, are _____perfect.

2. The amount of air in a football may be _____correct.

3. If you _____crease the amount of air, the ball is easier to grip.

4. Tampering with a game ball is highly _____honest.

5. Coaches cannot _____obey the rules.

6. Breaking the rules is an _____fortunate lapse in judgement.

7. Altering equipment may cause _____trust among sports fans.

8. Breaking the rules _____grades the reputation of the sport.

9. If a manager is _____certain, he or she must take action.

10. Teams must be careful, even if fans are _____patient for the game
    to begin.

____/10

Name _____ Date _____

Directions: Read the paragraph. For each sentence, write the correct prefix on the line to complete the word in the sentence.

il-	im-	in-	dis-	ir-	mis-	un-

When the spelling bee started, I was very confident. In fact,

I thought I was (1) _____capable of making a mistake. When it was my

turn, the judge said a word that was (2) _____familiar to me. I thought

perhaps she had (3) _____pronounced it. However, that kind of thinking

seemed highly (4) _____logical. I asked her to repeat the word, and she

did. I thought it would be (5) _____responsible or even

(6) _____polite to ask her to repeat it again. So I tried my best to spell the

word. But when I heard the buzzer, I knew that I had (7) _____spelled it.

I was so embarrassed I wanted to (8) _____appear! I guess when it comes

to spelling, I am (9) _____perfect after all. My dad said he might have to

(10) _____own me for getting a word wrong, but he was only joking.

_____/10

Name _____ Date _____

Directions: Read each sentence. Write the correct prefix from the box on the line to complete the word in the sentence.

il-	im-	in-	dis-	ir-	mis-	un-

1. At gymnastic meets, Liz is _____beaten in three events.

2. Her coach considers her _____replaceable on the gymnastic team.

3. She almost looks as if she is _____connected from gravity.

4. Liz's skill on the balance beam is almost _____logical.

5. As she performs, her smile is constant and _____resistible to her fans.

6. If she ever feels _____secure, no one can tell.

7. She shows no signs of _____balance as she spins and twirls.

8. Any mistakes are _____visible to the judges and the audience.

9. Her _____mounts are perfect, and the crowd always roars.

10. I have never seen her _____handle an opportunity to excel.

_____/10

Name _____ Date _____

Directions: Read the paragraph. For each sentence, write the correct prefix on the line to complete the word in the sentence.

pro-	em-	en-	per-	im-

My parents (1) _____mitted me to attend the Thanksgiving Day parade in our

town. This was the parade's first year, and it was an (2) _____mediate success. The

parade began at the library and (3) _____ceeded through town until it got to the

(4) _____trance to the community garden. The high school marching band

(5) _____formed popular show tunes. A group of jugglers (6) _____vided lively

entertainment and lots of laughs. An (7) _____mense float carried people dressed as

Pilgrims and Native Americans. A woman dressed as a pumpkin (8) _____chanted the

children. Then, a (9) _____cession of turkeys danced down the middle of the street.

Everyone in town seemed to (10) _____brace the idea of celebrating Thanksgiving with

a parade.

_____/10

Name _____ Date _____

Directions: Read each sentence and the three bold prefixes below the sentence. Circle the prefix that best fits in the blank to complete the word in the sentence.

1. Jessica's latest _____ject was building a model sailboat.

   per-   **pro-**   **im-**

2. She used some special wood _____ported from Brazil.

   per-   **im-**   **en-**

3. Jessica's parents _____migrated to the United States from Sri Lanka.

   im-   **en-**   **per-**

4. Jessica figured out about 80 _____cent of the directions by herself.

   im-   **en-**   **per-**

5. Using sandpaper _____abled her to shape and smooth the hull.

   per-   **im-**   **en-**

6. She _____bedded a GPS microchip in the hull of the boat.

   em-   **im-**   **en-**

7. Her father _____couraged her to take her time with the project.

   im-   **pro-**   **en-**

8. After weeks of work, she had _____duced a beautiful boat.

   im-   **en-**   **pro-**

_____/8

Name _____ Date _____

Directions: Read each sentence. Write the correct prefix from the box on the line to complete the word in the sentence.

trans-	per-	auto-	dec-

1. For more than six _____ ades, my grandfather has loved baseball.

2. All his life, he has been a _____petual fan.

3. He even has _____ graphs from famous baseball players.

4. "Baseball _____ ports me back to my childhood," he claims.

5. The back seat of his _____mobile was filled with boxes of baseball cards.

6. His favorite book is the _____biography of a former MVP with the New York Giants.

7. Last week he _____ferred his whole collection of cards to the basement.

8. If you invite him to a game, he'll say yes 100 _____cent of the time.

_____/8

Name _____ Date _____

Directions: Read the paragraph. For each sentence, write the correct prefix on the line to complete the word in the sentence.

trans-	per-	auto-	dec-

Carl opened his first savings account last week. He is happy that his

money will earn at least two (1) _____cent interest each month.

The bank allows the newspaper office to deposit his weekly paycheck

(2) _____matically. When he is old enough to have a checking account, it

will be easy to (3) _____fer money between the accounts. The bank makes

it easy to (4) _____form deposits and withdrawals. During one

(5) _____action, Carl made a funny mistake. He put the (6) _____imal

point in the wrong place and withdrew $60 instead of $6! Saving money

will (7) _____mit him to buy a car someday. Carl knows that if he (8)

_____sists in saving money, he'll have enough money to buy a car!

_____/8

Name _____ Date _____

Directions: Read each sentence. Write the correct prefix from the box on the line to complete the word in the sentence.

bi-	tri-	cent-	dec-	inter-	em-	ex-

1. A period of time between events is an _____val.

2. A _____enarian is a person who lives to be one hundred years old.

3. A _____pod has three legs and is used to hold a camera.

4. A road between states is an _____state highway.

5. The art of stitching decorations into cloth is _____broidery.

6. When you _____hale, you breathe air out.

7. A _____angle is a shape with three sides.

8. Saudi Arabia _____ports oil to many other countries.

9. A pair of _____focal glasses has two lenses.

10. Every public building must have an emergency _____it.

_____/10

Grades 3–6 • **Benchmark Advance** • **Phonics and Word Recognition** Quick Checks • © Benchmark Education Company, LLC

Name _____ Date _____

Directions: Read each sentence. Write the correct prefix from the box on the line to complete the word in the sentence.

| bi- | tri- | cent- | dec- | inter- | em- | ex- |

1. My family _____barked on a trip to Yellowstone National Park.

2. One day, we rode _____cycles to visit Old Faithful.

3. There, steam _____plodes from the ground many times a day.

4. The geyser erupts at _____vals between forty-five minutes and two hours.

5. If you are having a conversation, the geyser might _____rupt it.

6. The trip to Yellowstone _____ceeded my expectations.

7. People have been watching Old Faithful for more than a _____ury.

8. We passed around _____noculars so that everyone could see it better.

9. The steam can _____tend more than 150 feet into the air.

10. One man put his camera on a _____pod and took pictures of the geyser.

_____/10

Name _____ Date _____

Directions: Read each sentence and the three bold words below the sentence. Circle the form of the word that best fits in the blank to complete the sentence.

1. The _____ opened his shop at 6 a.m.

   baker   **bakor**   **baking**

2. The company president hired a _____ to take her to the airport.

   driver   **drivor**   **driving**

3. After publishing her first book, the _____ took some time off.

   writer   **writor**   **writing**

4. Many _____ used ships to travel to new lands.

   explorers   **explorors**   **exploring**

5. Every crane _____ must wear a hard hat on the construction site.

   operater   **operator**   **operating**

6. The _____ built simple wooden shelters.

   settlers   **settlors**   **settling**

7. The _____ to the city took the bus to the museum.

   visiters   **visitors**   **visiting**

8. That _____ won an award for his role in the movie.

   acter   **actor**   **acting**

_____/8

Name _____ Date _____

Directions: Read each sentence. Using one of the suffixes in the box, write the correct form of the bold word on the line to complete the sentence.

-er	-or

1. The _____ taught the class about Native American cultures.   **instruct**

2. The _____ cut a scene from the movie.   **produce**

3. After the train left the station, the _____ collected tickets.   **conduct**

4. The _____ visited a local elementary school.   **govern**

5. The _____ of the ship gave an order.   **command**

6. I enjoyed listening to the guest _____.   **speak**

7. The newspaper's _____ worked long hours at her job.   **edit**

8. Benjamin Franklin was a famous _____.   **invent**

9. Marc went to an _____ to help him manage his money.   **advise**

10. The _____ hurt his knee during the baseball game.   **catch**

____/10

Name _____ Date _____

Directions: Read each sentence. Write the correct suffix from the box on the line to complete the word in the sentence.

-ful	-able	-less

1. In August, we went camping at the wonder_____ Smith Forest.

2. The sky was bright blue and cloud_____ when we arrived.

3. We found a peace_____ place to set up our campsite.

4. The view of the lake nearby was remark_____.

5. My little sister was help_____ and gathered sticks for our campfire.

6. The leaves in the trees were motion_____ because there was no wind.

7. It started to rain, but our tent stayed dry and comfort_____.

8. After the rain ended, we saw a color_____ rainbow.

9. I saw a bug in our tent but my mom said it was harm_____.

10. We had an event_____ time camping together.

____/10

Name _____ Date _____

Directions: Read each sentence. Using one of the suffixes in the box, write the correct form of the bold word on the line to complete the sentence.

-ful	-able	-less

1. Our school's lacrosse team is very _____.   **success**

2. We were _____ that we'd win the next game.   **hope**

3. The other team seemed confident and _____.   **fear**

4. The tallest boy on the team is very _____ and   **power**
   scores a lot of points.

5. The nervousness on our team was _____.   **notice**

6. The players on the other team were more _____   **skill**
   than ours.

7. A game with a close score would have been _____.   **accept**

8. I twisted my ankle, and it was very _____.   **pain**

9. After putting ice on the ankle, the pain was _____.   **manage**

10. The game seemed _____ because we were   **end**
    losing badly.

____/10

Name _____ Date _____

Directions: Read each sentence. Write the correct suffix from the box on the line to complete the word in the sentence.

-ment	-ness

1. Much to our excite_____, our neighborhood has a new playground.

2. We ran up to the gate and looked at the playground with amaze_____.

3. The new equip_____ was very colorful and looked like fun.

4. My friends made an agree_____ that we would try out the slide first.

5. My little brother needed some encourage_____ to climb the wall.

6. The kids' loud_____ showed they were having fun.

7. We will certainly get hours of enjoy_____ from the playground.

8. I was surprised at the bold_____ of the little girl on the big slide.

9. The move_____ of the spinning tire made me feel dizzy.

10. The thick_____ of the ropes on the climbing structure was good.

___/10

Name _____ Date _____

Directions: Read each sentence. Using one of the suffixes in the box, write the correct form of the bold word on the line to complete the sentence.

-ment	-ness

1. We talked about the _____ of wind power in our area. **develop**

2. I fought my _____ during class and finished my work. **drowsy**

3. We got home just before _____ descended. **dark**

4. Trudy showed _____ when she played with the children. **kind**

5. Raffi proved his _____ by winning the 100-yard dash. **swift**

6. Project _____ is very important for a successful company. **manage**

7. The principal was proud of our school's _____ . **achieve**

8. We took a _____ of the plant's height in science class. **measure**

9. Jackson didn't have a single _____ in gym class. **weak**

10. The _____ of the sky that morning hurt my eyes. **bright**

____/10

Name _____ Date _____

Directions: Read each sentence. Write the correct suffix from the box on the line to complete the word in the sentence.

-ly	-ily	-ways	-wise

1. Near the pond, several children sat quiet_____.

2. We walked slow_____ so we didn't bother the birds.

3. The ducks looked at us and speed_____ swam away.

4. Like_____ the geese will swim away from us, because the ducks did.

5. Inside the nature center, I careful_____ picked up a small frog.

6. The live_____ gerbils ran back and forth in their cage.

7. The snakes slithered through the grass silent_____.

8. The turtles lazed about sleep_____ by the pond.

9. One lizard climbed side_____ up a tree.

10. The worker said the lizards are rare_____ awake during the day.

_____/10

Name _____ Date _____

Directions: Read each sentence. Using one of the suffixes in the box, write the correct form of the bold word on the line to complete the sentence.

-ly	-ily	-ways	-wise

1. We lined up _____ beside the buses for our field trip to Washington, D.C.   **length**

2. The students listened _____ to the first speaker.   **eager**

3. The students _____ paid the bus fare.   **willing**

4. More than 100 students _____ boarded the buses and got ready to go.   **rapid**

5. Some students grumbled _____ when Mr. Freeman said we had to leave at 6 a.m.   **unhappy**

6. _____, everyone was excited about the trip.   **other**

7. During the trip, I sat _____ so I could look out the window.   **side**

8. Mom cut my sandwich _____ into little strips.   **cross**

9. Max _____ ate all my snacks without asking me.   **greed**

10. When we got to the memorial, we walked around it _____.   **clock**

____/10

Name _____ Date _____

Directions: Read each sentence. Write the correct suffix from the box on the line to complete the word in the sentence.

-ful	-ous	-ible	-able	-some

1. A marvel_____ animal expert spoke to our class.

2. He was knowledge_____ about many types of animals and insects.

3. We learned that a scorpion sting is poison_____.

4. The colors of the poison dart frog are really awe_____.

5. Badgers are danger_____ animals that will attack people.

6. He said a spider bite can be quite pain_____.

7. The black widow has a notice_____ red mark on its back.

8. An owl's neck is flex_____ and can turn in a full circle.

9. The sloth is comfort_____ sitting in a tree all day long.

10. Lectures can be tire_____, but this one was really exciting.

_____/10

Name _____ Date _____

Directions: Read each sentence. Using one of the suffixes in the box, write the correct form of the bold word on the line to complete the sentence.

-ful	-ous	-ible	-able	-some

1. During the summer, going to the beach is _____.   **enjoy**

2. The sunny weather makes me feel _____.   **cheer**

3. It is _____ that we will catch the bus.   **doubt**

4. I am a _____ swimmer and never go out too far.   **caution**

5. Most of the birds at the beach are _____.   **recognize**

6. Seeing a whale come to the surface is a _____ sight.   **wonder**

7. We had 20 people for a game, and 20 is _____ by 4.   **divide**

8. Watching out for jellyfish can be _____.   **trouble**

9. At the end of the day, the sunset was _____.   **glory**

10. I get _____ sitting on the beach by myself.   **lone**

_____/10

Name _____ Date _____

Directions: Read each sentence. Write the correct suffix from the box on the line to complete the word in the sentence.

-ous	-ive	-able	-ial	-al	-less

1. Our family adopted a very act_____ puppy.

2. I'm convinced that we have a very spec_____ pet.

3. Puppies can be destruct_____, so we have to watch him carefully.

4. I told my mother I am depend_____ and will walk the puppy every day.

5. It is humor_____ to see the puppy chase after birds in our yard.

6. We may need to bring the puppy to a profession_____ trainer.

7. My dad thinks my brother and I need parent_____ help with the puppy.

8. The puppy has destroyed count_____ plastic toys.

9. I'm usually breath_____ from trying to chase him.

10. It is understand_____ that my parents want me to help feed him.

____/10

Name _____ Date _____

Directions: Read each sentence. Using one of the suffixes in the box, write the correct form of the bold word on the line to complete the sentence.

-ous	-ive	-able	-ial	-al	-less

1. Billy read a book about a man's _____ climb up Mt. Everest.   **peril**

2. The climb was made for both scientific and _____ purposes.   **commerce**

3. The leader of the group seemed mean and _____.   **heart**

4. Billy couldn't imagine a _____ uphill climb for two months.   **labor**

5. The mountain is one of the world's _____ wonders.   **nature**

6. There have been a few _____ disappearances on the trail.   **mystery**

7. The weather is not _____ and can change within minutes.   **predict**

8. The man's journey hardly seemed _____ because it was so difficult.   **believe**

9. Billy is _____ and would like to climb a mountain one day.   **adventure**

10. Some climbers need _____ help after such a difficult trek.   **medic**

____/10

Name _____ Date _____

Directions: Read each sentence. Write the correct suffix from the box on the line to complete the word in the sentence.

-y	-ent	-ive	-ic	-ful

1. On rain_____ days, we do not go outside for recess.

2. Our art teacher is invent_____ and comes up with exciting projects.

3. The athlet_____ fields have brand new grass.

4. My social studies teacher tells us about histor_____ places.

5. Our gym teacher makes sure we stay act_____ during her class.

6. School gets canceled when the weather is snow_____.

7. Our art teacher says it's okay to get mess_____.

8. I feel confid_____ when I answer a question in math class.

9. We read a book that uses poet_____ language.

10. When the school fire alarm sounds, it is urg_____ to get outside quickly.

_____/10

Name _____ Date _____

Directions: Read each sentence. Using one of the suffixes in the box, write the correct form of the bold word on the line to complete the sentence.

-y	-ent	-ive	-ic	-ful

1. Mrs. Johansen is a _____ gardener.　　**master**

2. When Mrs. Johansen first started gardening, she had to learn _____ facts about plants.　　**base**

3. She thinks of gardening as a _____ and rewarding hobby.　　**meaning**

4. She plants _____ flowers along the sides of the garden pathway.　　**attract**

5. Every year she plants _____ kinds of vegetables.　　**differ**

6. She likes flowers that have a _____ smell.　　**fruit**

7. If there are too many _____ days, the plants will grow slowly.　　**cloud**

8. Some vegetables will not grow in _____ soil.　　**acid**

9. Mrs. Johansen and her family have _____ fresh vegetables to eat.　　**delight**

10. It takes a _____ person to be a gardener.　　**patience**

____/10

Name _____ Date _____

Directions: Read each sentence. Write the correct suffix from the box on the line to complete the word in the sentence.

-dom	-ity	-tion	-ment	-ness	-ism

1. The king_____ would soon have a new ruler.

2. The people greeted the news with a sense of excite_____.

3. Queen Regina has promised free_____ for all people in the land.

4. Queen Regina is appreciated for her kind_____ and patience.

5. Magicians and other performers provided entertain_____ at the ceremony.

6. Other impressive castles in the area improved tour_____ and attracted visitors.

7. To the people's amaze_____, the queen shook everyone's hand.

8. The queen's leadership and ideal_____ will bring a welcome change.

9. The queen is known for her generos____ and helps people in need.

10. Many people will pay close atten_____ to the decisions she makes.

_____/10

Name _____ Date _____

Directions: Read each sentence. Using one of the suffixes in the box, write the correct form of the bold word on the line to complete the sentence.

-dom	-ity	-tion	-ment	-ness	-ism

1. I read about a dog that showed _____ **hero**
   by rescuing a little boy.

2. After much _____, we decided to adopt a dog **consider**
   named Stella.

3. Having a dog around the house has become a **real**

   _____.

4. I never knew a puppy could have such _____. **wild**

5. It is my _____ to walk Stella every day. **responsible**

6. Stella's clumsy _____ is so funny to watch. **move**

7. Stella has achieved _____ in our neighborhood; **star**
   everyone knows her.

8. Stella's one _____ is climbing stairs, but she'll **weak**
   figure it out.

9. Professional training is not a _____, but it's a **require**
   good idea.

10. Stella is a wonderful _____ to our family. **add**

____/10

Name _____ Date _____

Directions: Read each sentence. Write the correct suffix from the box on the line to complete the word in the sentence.

-ology	-ant	-er	-ist	-or	-ery

1. Bio_____ is the study of animals.

2. Morton is an attend_____ in Dr. Geller's lab.

3. Morton is also a great scient_____.

4. Dr. Geller hired a new assist_____ to help with the study.

5. Dr. Geller is the direct_____ of the program.

6. When he is not working, Morton practices arch_____.

7. A journal_____ wrote about the study in the newspaper.

8. Some clever animals used trick_____ to get more food.

9. Dr. Geller is also an expert in meteor_____.

10. The profess_____ presented the results in class.

____/10

Name _____ Date _____

Directions: Read each sentence. Using one of the suffixes in the box, write the correct form of the bold word on the line to complete the sentence.

-ology	-ant	-er	-ist	-or	-ery

1. I read a book about Greek _____ after I learned about the Greek gods in class.   **myth**

2. On the first day, a sidewalk _____ drew my picture.   **art**

3. We greeted the _____ from the meeting earlier that day.   **participate**

4. The woman is a _____ who recreates famous buildings in her paintings.   **paint**

5. Mr. Maxwell is a _____ of rare coins.   **collect**

6. One _____ stopped at a booth and bought a rug.   **custom**

7. Victor worked as a _____ in a restaurant.   **serve**

8. Two women were selling some beautiful rolls outside the _____.   **bake**

_____/8

Name _____ Date _____

Directions: Read each sentence. Write the correct suffix from the box on the line to complete the word in the sentence.

-tion	-ty	-sion	-ness	-ment

1. In ancient Japan, loyal_____ was very important.

2. A valuable servant showed devo_____ to his master.

3. In the emperor's court, people were expected to show polite_____ at all times.

4. Performers came to the court for the ruler's amuse_____.

5. Visitors from other lands were viewed with fascina_____.

6. Sometimes, there was ten_____ between rival families.

7. The emperor and his wife were models of refine_____ and grace.

8. The crown was a symbol of royal_____.

9. Warriors achieved great_____ by fighting for their lords.

10. Some warriors gained permis_____ to travel to other lands.

_____/10

Name _____ Date _____

Directions: Read each sentence. Using one of the suffixes in the box, write the correct form of the bold word on the line to complete the sentence.

-tion	-ty	-sion	-ness	-ment

1. My _____ was placed on display in the library. **create**

2. I believe that _____ is important when making art. **honest**

3. As _____ for my work, I drew the design on paper first. **prepare**

4. I get a feeling of _____ from working on a sculpture. **content**

5. Out of _____, I had to work faster than I usually do. **necessary**

6. I faced some _____ in trying to finish the piece on time. **difficult**

7. Sometimes, other artists feel _____ when they see a great work. **resent**

8. After the show, we held a _____ about art. **discuss**

9. It is fun to watch a person's _____ when he or she sees my work. **react**

10. One person stared at my sculpture with a look of _____. **astonish**

____/10

Name _____ Date _____

Directions: Read each sentence. Using the information in the chart, write the meaning of the underlined word in the sentence on the line.

Greek and Latin Roots	Meaning
archae	ancient
geo	Earth
rupt	break
ology	study of

1. Peter decided to <u>interrupt</u> our conversation.

_____

2. Ms. Hallstrom is a <u>geologist</u>.

_____

3. Her closest friend works in <u>archaeology</u>.

_____

4. She used the laws of <u>geology</u> to find the location of a hidden temple.

_____

5. The words on the tomb were written in an <u>archaic</u> language.

_____

6. A volcano near the temple <u>erupted</u> less than a year ago.

_____

____/6

Name _____ Date _____

Directions: Read each sentence. Using the information in the chart, write the meaning of the underlined word in the sentence on the line.

Greek and Latin Roots	Meaning
archae	ancient
geo	Earth
rupt	break
ology	study of

1. Mr. Vespa specializes in <u>geothermal</u> heat systems for people's homes.

_____

2. He checks <u>archaeological</u> studies of the area before he starts digging a foundation.

_____

3. Unfortunately, last year his company went <u>bankrupt</u>.

_____

4. An <u>archaeologist</u> found evidence of Native American settlements near a city in New Mexico.

_____

5. Mr. Vespa had bought the land and hired a <u>geographer</u> to map the area.

_____

6. His plan to build a housing development came to an <u>abrupt</u> end.

_____

_____/6

Name _____ Date _____

Directions: Read each sentence. Using the information in the chart, write the meaning of the underlined word in the sentence on the line.

Greek and Latin Roots	Meaning
agri	field
duc, duct	to lead
man	hand
mis	to send

1. Ms. Barton decided to <u>dismiss</u> the class early.

_____

2. The principal will <u>conduct</u> an inspection of the school's heating system.

_____

3. One company in California <u>manufactures</u> solar panels for schools.

_____

4. Mrs. Cinque's goal is to <u>educate</u> children in the wonders of music.

_____

5. We were on a <u>mission</u> to find the hamster that had escaped.

_____

6. Mr. Fuentes plans to teach our class about <u>agribusiness</u>.

_____

_____/6

Name _____ Date _____

Directions: Read each sentence. Using the information in the chart, write the meaning of the underlined word in the sentence on the line.

Greek and Latin Roots	Meaning
agri	field
duc, duct	to lead
man	hand
mis	to send

1. Father Bartolo was a <u>missionary</u> who traveled to the New World.

_____

2. He knew that <u>agriculture</u> would be important in California.

_____

3. In one area, he designed and built an <u>aqueduct</u> to help the farmers.

_____

4. He hired dozens of <u>manual</u> laborers to work on the farm.

_____

5. One day, Father Bartolo received a <u>missive</u> from the King of Spain.

_____

6. He wanted to <u>induce</u> the local people to become loyal subjects of Spain.

_____

_____/6

Name _____ Date _____

Directions: Read each sentence. Using the information in the chart, write the meaning of the underlined word in the sentence on the line.

Greek and Latin Roots	Meaning
graph	to write
migr	to move
mit	to send
ven	to come

1. Samuel Morse made the first <u>telegraph</u> in 1838.

_____

2. He also <u>invented</u> a code using dots and dashes.

_____

3. It allowed people to <u>transmit</u> messages over a wire.

_____

4. After the railroad was built, thousands of Americans <u>migrated</u> west.

_____

5. A member of Congress <u>submitted</u> a bill to form two new states.

_____

6. Other members of Congress tried to <u>prevent</u> that from happening.

_____

_____/6

Name _____ Date _____

Directions: Read each sentence. Using the information in the chart, write the meaning of the underlined word in the sentence on the line.

Greek and Latin Roots	Meaning
graph	to write
migr	to move
mit	to send
ven	to come

1. A number of local leaders <u>convened</u> at City Hall.

_____

2. A person on the street asked Mayor Sanders for an <u>autograph</u>.

_____

3. Hundreds of <u>immigrants</u> have arrived from the Middle East.

_____

4. The U.S. government <u>admitted</u> more than a thousand refugees.

_____

5. The mayor chose the school auditorium as the <u>venue</u> for the meeting.

_____

6. He hired a <u>graphic</u> artist to make some official signs.

_____

____/6

Name _____ Date _____

Directions: Read each sentence. Using the information in the chart, write the meaning of the underlined word in the sentence on the line.

Greek and Latin Roots	Meaning
aud	to hear
liter	letters
spec	to see
struct	to build
vent	to come
graphy	writing, showing

1. Our teacher, Ms. Pulaski, went to a <u>convention</u> last week.

_____

2. The main topic was world <u>literacy</u>.

_____

3. The first speaker was barely <u>audible</u>.

_____

4. We will <u>construct</u> a birdhouse to feed the birds that visit us.

_____

5. We also need to <u>respect</u> the fact that people have different strengths.

_____

6. Marcie took <u>photography</u> classes as part of her summer school assignment.

_____

____/6

Name _____ Date _____

Directions: Read each sentence. Using the information in the chart, write the meaning of the underlined word in the sentence on the line.

Greek and Latin Roots	Meaning
aud	to hear
liter	letters
spec	to see
struct	to build
vent	to come
graphy	writing, showing

1. An earthquake caused the <u>destruction</u> of some ancient ruins.

_____

2. Scientists studied <u>geography</u> to determine the damage of the earthquake.

_____

3. Experts in ancient history conservation went to <u>inspect</u> the ruins.

_____

4. To the scientists' disappointment, only one <u>structure</u> was still standing.

_____

5. An archaeologist taped an <u>audio</u> presentation about the project.

_____

6. Many of the buildings were described in <u>literature</u> from long ago.

_____

____/6

Name _____ Date _____

Directions: Read each sentence. Using the information in the chart, write the meaning of the underlined word in the sentence on the line.

Greek and Latin Roots	Meaning
aud	to hear
cede	to go or yield
form	shape
vis	to see
graphic	written or shown in some way

1. My brother Dean went to the community college to <u>audit</u> a class.

_____

2. He wants to study the <u>visual</u> arts when he graduates from high school.

_____

3. A few simple lines can <u>transform</u> a picture.

_____

4. Dean thinks he can <u>succeed</u> in his new job as an artist.

_____

5. He says he can make ideas and beliefs <u>visible</u> to everyone.

_____

6. Dean did a lot of research for his <u>infographic</u> about colors and shapes.

_____

____/6

Name _____ Date _____

Directions: Read each sentence. Using the information in the chart, write the meaning of the underlined word in the sentence on the line.

Greek and Latin Roots	Meaning
aud	to hear
cede	to go or yield
form	shape
vis	to see
graphic	written or shown in some way

1. In the book, the main character says that he can make himself <u>invisible</u>.

_____

2. Then he <u>proceeds</u> to disappear from sight.

_____

3. Nothing the main character does <u>conforms</u> with the laws of physics.

_____

4. Last night, I <u>exceeded</u> the amount of time I planned to spend reading.

_____

5. If I can get this book on tape, I would enjoy the <u>auditory</u> parts of the story, such as the dialogue.

_____

6. Reading this book has <u>reformed</u> my view of reading for fun.

_____

____/6

Name _____ Date _____

Directions: Read each sentence. Using the information in the chart, write the meaning of the underlined word in the sentence on the line.

Greek and Latin Roots	Meaning
ang	to bend
cline	to lean
mech	machine
mot	to move
struct	to build
scope	an instrument used to view or observe

1. Every year, Ariana and her brother <u>construct</u> a car for the soapbox derby.

_____

2. Ariana has a <u>mechanical</u> engineering degree.

_____

3. Her brother makes an <u>inclined</u> ramp where they can test the car.

_____

4. A soapbox derby car must run without a <u>motor</u>.

_____

5. Their car has an <u>angular</u> shape to make it run faster.

_____

6. Ariana and her brother do not need a <u>microscope</u> to fix the steering wheel.

_____

_____/6

Name _____ Date _____

Directions: Read each sentence. Using the information in the chart, write the meaning of the underlined word in the sentence on the line.

Greek and Latin Roots	Meaning
ang	bend
cline	lean
mech	machine
mot	move
struct	build
scope	an instrument used to view or observe

1. Luke invented a <u>mechanism</u> that sees around corners.

_____

2. The main <u>structure</u> of the device is a set of tubes.

_____

3. Inside the tubes are some mirrors set at different <u>angles</u>.

_____

4. He likes to <u>recline</u> on the couch and think up new ideas.

_____

5. Luke also likes to see the stars through his <u>telescope</u>.

_____

6. Luke wants to <u>promote</u> the use of science in everyday life.

_____

_____/6

Name _____ Date _____

Directions: Read each sentence. Using the information in the chart, write the meaning of the underlined word in the sentence on the line.

Greek Science Roots	Meaning
atmo	air; vapor
bio	life
hydro	water
photo	light
phobia	fear

1. My dad's company built a <u>biodome</u> in the mountains.

_____

2. The building has its own <u>atmosphere</u>.

_____

3. He showed me a <u>photograph</u> of the building.

_____

4. A wheel inside the dome produces <u>hydroelectricity</u>.

_____

5. People inside the dome cannot have <u>claustrophobia</u>.

_____

6. The roof of the dome is covered with <u>photoelectric</u> cells.

_____

____/6

Name _____ Date _____

Directions: Read each sentence. Using the information in the chart, write the meaning of the underlined word in the sentence on the line.

Greek Science Roots	Meaning
atmo	air; vapor
bio	life
hydro	water
photo	light
phobia	fear

1. Marco used a <u>telephoto</u> lens to take a picture.

_____

2. There is a red <u>hydrant</u> on the sidewalk in front of the building.

_____

3. One scientist used an <u>atmometer</u> to collect information.

_____

4. The city wants to use <u>biofuel</u> to produce electricity.

_____

5. Kevin has had <u>arachnophobia</u> since he was bitten by a spider.

_____

6. We can make a <u>photocopy</u> of this map showing where the wells are.

_____

_____/6

Name _____ Date _____

Directions: Read each sentence. Using the information in the chart, write the meaning of the underlined word in the sentence on the line.

Greek and Latin Roots	Meaning
amphi	around
aqua	water
fac	make; do
grat	pleasing
luna	moon
anti	against

1. Ms. Laporte studies <u>aquatic</u> animals.

_____

2. She gave a presentation in the <u>amphitheater</u>.

_____

3. The ocean tides are affected by <u>lunar</u> movement.

_____

4. Learning about fascinating animals is <u>gratifying</u> to me.

_____

5. Ms. Laporte invented a new <u>antibiotic</u> to kill germs.

_____

6. She wants to open a small <u>factory</u> to produce her invention.

_____

____/6

Name _____ Date _____

Directions: Read each sentence. Using the information in the chart, write the meaning of the underlined word in the sentence on the line.

Greek and Latin Roots	Meaning
amphi	around
aqua	water
fac	make; do
grat	pleasing
luna	moon
anti	against

1. Lucy and I found an <u>amphibian</u> in the weeds by the river.

_____

2. We brought the animal to our school <u>aquatic</u> center where we study marine life.

_____

3. Lucy wants to have a paper <u>facsimile</u> of the animal for our project.

_____

4. I expressed my <u>gratitude</u> for her help on the project.

_____

5. We studied <u>lunar</u> eclipse in astronomy class and saw it through our class telescope.

_____

6. Our astronomy lab is a great <u>facility</u> for viewing the night sky.

_____

____/6

Name _____ Date _____

Directions: Read each sentence. Using the information in the chart, write the meaning of the underlined word in the sentence on the line.

Latin Roots	Meaning
dorm	sleep
inter	between
sub	below
sur	above
vis	sight

1. Dr. Gallant dreams of <u>interplanetary</u> travel.

_____

2. He has analyzed dust and rocks from the <u>surface</u> of the moon.

_____

3. He wants to <u>supervise</u> a team of scientists.

_____

4. He thinks there might be <u>dormant</u> bacteria in the soil on Mars.

_____

5. Sometimes he has to use <u>substandard</u> equipment.

_____

6. He wrote an <u>interoffice</u> memo last week to complain.

_____

_____/6

Name _____ Date _____

Directions: Read each sentence. Using the information in the chart, write the meaning of the underlined word in the sentence on the line.

Latin Roots	Meaning
dorm	sleep
inter	between
sub	below
sur	above
vis	sight

1. The city of Montreal has a good <u>subway</u> system.

_____

2. The Canadian government charges a <u>surtax</u> on gasoline and other goods.

_____

3. On our trip to Montreal, we stayed in a <u>dormitory</u> for students.

_____

4. Charles is worried that his <u>vision</u> is getting weaker.

_____

5. We crossed an <u>international</u> border on our way to Montreal.

_____

6. Charles noticed a <u>surcharge</u> on our bill at the hotels.

_____

____/6

Quick Check #1
1. sing
2. game
3. cane
4. jest
5. kite
6. rice
7. shrug
8. jade

Quick Check #2
1. page
2. call
3. hinge
4. braces
5. cold
6. since
7. sold
8. blog

Quick Check #3
1. knife
2. wring
3. whole
4. note
5. root
6. beat
7. noose
8. whim

Quick Check #4
1. know
2. wrap
3. gnome
4. dough
5. knock
6. whose
7. wrist
8. sign

Quick Check #5
1. cab
2. branch
3. pane
4. black
5. fat
6. tape
7. lash
8. gram

Quick Check #6
1. band
2. mad
3. shack
4. tack
5. ant
6. sack
7. grand
8. ax

Quick Check #7
1. lick
2. sit
3. pine
4. bring
5. mile
6. dim
7. slid
8. chin

Quick Check #8
1. pick
2. mitt
3. will
4. rid
5. win
6. fill
7. twin
8. string

Quick Check #9
1. odd
2. cone
3. got
4. stock
5. pop
6. note
7. jock
8. mod

Quick Check #10
1. rod
2. hot
3. sob
4. shop
5. cop
6. lock
7. fond
8. long

Quick Check #11
1. went
2. bet
3. she
4. step
5. pep
6. bell
7. jest
8. left

Quick Check #12
1. get
2. then
3. set
4. fed
5. send
6. met
7. went
8. fell

Quick Check #13
1. mutt
2. cub
3. stun
4. chuck
5. lug
6. mule
7. fuss
8. dud

Quick Check #14
1. us
2. hunk
3. must
4. run
5. nut
6. bunt
7. cut
8. pump

Quick Check #15
(Student reads words aloud.)
Words with the long vowel *a* sound: escape, playpen, basement, relay, painter, grain, gateway

Quick Check #16
(Student reads words aloud.)
Words with the long vowel *a* sound: gray, race, wake, replace, faint, training, afraid, lazy, maybe

Quick Check #17
(Student reads words aloud.)
Words with the long vowel *i* sound: bride, driver, pilot, silent, unties, fight, reply, time, describe

Quick Check #18
(Student reads words aloud.)
Words with the long vowel *i* sound: sideline, white, twice, highlight, tonight, kind, pilot, refried, retry

Quick Check #19
(Student reads words aloud.)
Words with the long vowel *o* sound: stove, snowfall, soapstone, below, alone, polo, hopeful, bowling, remote, whole

Quick Check #20
(Student reads words aloud.)
Words with the long vowel *o* sound: grown, showman, throat, homeland, awoke, open, solo, explode, token, coatcheck

Quick Check #21
(Student reads words aloud.)
Words with the long vowel *e* sound: cheat, sweetly, greet, these valley, keyhole, peanut, fleece, fifteen

Quick Check #22
(Student reads words aloud.)
Words with the long vowel *e* sound: wheat, beet, leaf, street, cheese, steeply, breathe, pleasing, treetop, breeze

Quick Check #23
(Student reads words aloud.)
Words with the /är/ sound: harvest, sparkle, marble, barber, remark, farmer, cartoon, guitar, garden, artist

Quick Check #24
(Student reads words aloud.)
Words with the /är/ sound: yarn, heart, scarlet, apartment, marble, garbage, pardon, alarm

Quick Check #25
(Student reads words aloud.)
Words with the /ôr/ sound: afford, ignore, report, outdoor, coral, forest, hornet, popcorn, explore, morning

Quick Check #26
(Student reads words aloud.)
Words with the /ôr/ sound: before, forget, tornado, storm, orbit, discord, roar, corner

Quick Check #27
(Student reads words aloud.)
Words with the /ûr/ sound: adventure, hurdle, nursery, pearl, third, murmur, picture, mercy, curtain, furnace

Quick Check #28
(Student reads words aloud.)
Words with the /ûr/ sound: sherbet, curtail, thirsty, purple, firm, occurred, sturdy, circle

Quick Check #29
(Student reads words aloud.)
Words with the /ir/ sound: clear, reindeer, career, interfere, atmosphere, disappear, engineer, weary, revered, year

Quick Check #30
(Student reads words aloud.)
Words with the /ir/ sound: earnest, dreary, cheerful, appear, sincere, beard, volunteer, smear, pioneer

Quick Check #31
(Student reads words aloud.)
Words with the /ar/ sound: hair, compare, software, square, careful, beware, dairy, airport, glare, repair

Quick Check #32
(Student reads words aloud.)
Words with the /ar/ sound: prepare, care, downstairs, share, flare, prairie, fair, declare

Quick Check #33
(Student reads words aloud.)
Words with the /ar/ sound: everywhere, therefore, where, swear, somewhere, bear

Quick Check #34
(Student reads words aloud.)
Words with the /ar/ sound: fear, shear, swear, steer, there, here

Quick Check #35
(Student reads words aloud.)
Words with the /ou/ sound: crowd, house, down, tower, mountain, brown, towel, prowl, shower, shout

Quick Check #36
(Student reads words aloud.)
Words with the /ou/ sound: proud, blouse, sound, spout, doubt, ground, snout, about, sprout

Quick Check #37
(Student reads words aloud.)
Words with the /oi/ sound: spoil, soil, voice, joint, destroy, toil, point, noise, boil, annoy

Quick Check #38
(Student reads words aloud.)
Words with the /oi/ sound: join, coin, royalty, toys, joyful, coil, employ, choice, moist, hoist

Quick Check #39
(Student reads words aloud.)
Words with the /o͞o/ sound: fool, group, juice, shoe, fruit, hoop, troop, goose, you, canoe

Quick Check #40
(Student reads words aloud.)
Words with the /o͞o/ sound: soup, raccoon, groom, through, bloom, suit, hoot, loose, mousse

Quick Check #41
(Student reads words aloud.)
Words with the /o͝o/ sound: could, wooden, hood, look, good, wood, took, would, cook

Quick Check #42
(Student reads words aloud.)
Words with the /o͝o/ sound: stood, should, shook, swoosh, goodbye, rookie, woolen, brook, nook, understood

Quick Check #43
(Student reads words aloud.)
Syllables:

be|cause	aw|ful	al|ways
wal|let	al|so	with|draw
au|thor	hal|ter	fal|ling
hau|ling	sau|sage	smal|ler

Quick Check #44
(Student reads words aloud.)
Syllables:

law|ful	draw|ing	launch|pad
fault|less	paus|ing	daugh|ter
dry|wall	craw|ling	hall|way
al|most	cole|slaw	cau|tion

Quick Check #45
(Student reads words aloud.)
Syllables:

ab|sent	ten|nis	com|et
vel|vet	mag|net	hap|pen
tun|nel	chan|nel	pil|grim
but|ton	fab|ric	cac|tus

Quick Check #46
(Student reads words aloud.)
Syllables:

con|trast	trum|pet	bank|rupt
wis|dom	mam|mal	hun|dred
blos|som	pub|lish	com|bat
splen|did	con|gress	cus|tom

Quick Check #47
(Student reads words aloud.)
Syllables:

pi|lot	to|tal	fe|ver
po|ny	e|vent	ze|ro
lo|cal	mi|nus	ba|con
na|vy	a|ble	re|mind

Quick Check #48
(Student reads words aloud.)
Syllables:

re|mit	ci|der	mi|nor
slo|gan	tro|phy	ro|tate
me|ter	bru|tal	va|cant
i|vy	mo|ment	fre|quent

Quick Check #49
(Student reads words aloud.)
Syllables:

tick|le	mar|ble	un|cle
set|tle	ea|gle	no|ble
an|kle	bun|dle	nee|dle
can|dle	tem|ple	bot|tle

Quick Check #50
(Student reads words aloud.)
Syllables:

sen|si|ble	pick|le	strug|gle
throt|tle	en|ti|tle	as|sem|ble
re|sem|ble	tan|gle	mul|ti|ple
mum|ble	par|ti|cle	vis|i|ble

Quick Check #51
(Student reads words aloud.)
Syllables:

a|head	dead|ly	soa|py
wea|ther	sound|ed	cer|tain
break|fast	dead|line	feath|er
squeal|ing	pea|nut	taint|ed

Quick Check #52
(Student reads words aloud.)
Syllables:

health|y	frown|ing	por|trait
round|ed	plea|sure	meat|ball
spoil|age	cur|tain	goal|ie
fur|i|ous	clown|ing	jeal|ous

Quick Check #53
(Student reads words aloud.)
Syllables:

de|cline	ar|rive	be|have
mis|spoke	pro|pose	ex|cite
re|pave	in|vite	en|grave
re|mote	re|fute	re|state

Quick Check #54
(Student reads words aloud.)
Syllables:

mis|take	vi|brate	be|spoke
de|mote	de|prive	re|pute
mu|tate	im|pose	snow|flake
con|fine	sim|u|late	al|pine

Grades 3–6 • Benchmark Advance • **Phonics and Word Recognition** Quick Checks • © Benchmark Education Company, LLC

Quick Check #55
(Student reads words aloud.)
Syllables:

curl|ing	dis|turb	com|pare
firm|ly	cur|sive	cur|rent
be|ware	ther|mos	sur|prise
ver|bal	por|ches	her|mit

Quick Check #56
(Student reads words aloud.)
Syllables:

pur|chase	e|merge	por|cu|pine
in|spect|or	jour|nal	sur|round
ver|sus	sur|ren|der	sir|loin
sur|vi|val	re|morse	or|gan|ize

Quick Check #57
1. dishwasher   dish washer
2. downstairs   down stairs
3. sunlight   sun light
4. backyard   back yard
5. flashlight   flash light
6. necklace   neck lace
7. airplane   air plane
8. headphones   head phones
9. courthouse   court house
10. teammate   team mate

Quick Check #58
1. steps
2. out
3. along
4. over
5. room
6. glasses
7. light
8. coat

Quick Check #59
1. placed
2. blasted
3. carrying
4. waving
5. bumped
6. skating
7. constructed
8. motioned

Quick Check #60
1. assisted
2. creating
3. denied
4. limping
5. tidied
6. arrived
7. responding
8. mixed
9. fighting

Quick Check #61
1. knives
2. sheep
3. halves
4. volcanoes
5. calves
6. wolves
7. feet
8. shelves

Quick Check #62
1. elves
2. loaves
3. cacti
4. children
5. tomatoes
6. bison
7. echoes
8. deer
9. potatoes
10. hooves

Quick Check #63
1. dislikes
2. unhealthy
3. disagree
4. disappear
5. unable
6. uncommon
7. discovers
8. uncertain

Quick Check #64
1. dis-
2. un-
3. un-
4. dis-
5. dis-
6. un-
7. un-
8. un-
9. dis-
10. dis-

Quick Check #65
1. preschool
2. preplanned
3. reviewed
4. preheated
5. reopened
6. recycle
7. revisit
8. recall

Quick Check #66
1. pre-
2. re-
3. re-
4. re-
5. pre-
6. re-
7. re-
8. re-

Quick Check #67
1. sub-
2. trans-
3. pro-
4. super-
5. inter-
6. pro-
7. trans-
8. inter-

Quick Check #68
1. inter-
2. sub-
3. trans-
4. pro-
5. inter-
6. super-
7. trans-
8. pro-
9. super-
10. super-

Quick Check #69
1. dis-
2. de-
3. im-
4. un-
5. de-
6. de-
7. dis-
8. in-

Quick Check #70
1. im-
2. in-
3. de-
4. dis-
5. dis-
6. un-
7. dis-
8. de-
9. un-
10. im-

Quick Check #71
1. in-
2. un-
3. mis-
4. il-
5. ir-
6. im-
7. mis-
8. dis-
9. im-
10. dis-

Quick Check #72
1. un-
2. ir-
3. dis-
4. il-
5. ir-
6. in-
7. im-
8. in-
9. dis-
10. mis-

Quick Check #73
1. per-
2. im-
3. pro-
4. en-
5. per-
6. pro-
7. im-
8. en-
9. pro-
10. em-

Quick Check #74
1. pro-
2. im-
3. im-
4. per-
5. en-
6. em-
7. en-
8. pro-

Quick Check #75
1. dec-
2. per-
3. auto-
4. trans-
5. auto-
6. auto-
7. trans-
8. per-

Quick Check #76
1. per-
2. auto-
3. trans-
4. per-
5. trans-
6. dec-
7. per-
8. per-

Quick Check #77
1. inter-
2. cent-
3. tri-
4. inter-
5. em-
6. ex-
7. tri-
8. ex-
9. bi-
10. ex-

Quick Check #78
1. em-
2. bi-
3. ex-
4. inter-
5. inter-
6. ex-
7. cent-
8. bi-
9. ex-
10. tri-

Quick Check #79
1. baker
2. driver
3. writer
4. explorers
5. operator
6. settlers
7. visitors
8. actor

Quick Check #80
1. instructor
2. producer
3. conductor
4. governor
5. commander
6. speaker
7. editor
8. inventor
9. advisor
10. catcher

Quick Check #81
1. -ful
2. -less
3. -ful
4. -able
5. -ful
6. -less
7. -able
8. -ful
9. -less
10. -ful

Quick Check #82
1. successful
2. hopeful
3. fearless
4. powerful
5. noticeable
6. skillful
7. acceptable
8. painful
9. manageable
10. endless

Quick Check #83
1. -ment
2. -ment
3. -ment
4. -ment
5. -ment
6. -ness
7. -ment
8. -ness
9. -ment
10. -ness

Quick Check #84
1. development
2. drowsiness
3. darkness
4. kindness
5. swiftness
6. management
7. achievement
8. measurement
9. weakness
10. brightness

Quick Check #85
1. -ly
2. -ly
3. -ily
4. -wise
5. -ly
6. -ly
7. -ly
8. -ily
9. -ways
10. -ly

Quick Check #86
1. lengthwise
2. eagerly
3. willingly
4. rapidly
5. unhappily
6. Otherwise
7. sideways
8. crosswise
9. greedily
10. clockwise

Quick Check #87
1. -ous
2. -able
3. -ous
4. -some
5. -ous
6. -ful
7. -able
8. -ible
9. -able
10. -some

Quick Check #88
1. enjoyable
2. cheerful
3. doubtful
4. cautious
5. recognizable
6. wonderful
7. divisible
8. troublesome
9. glorious
10. lonesome

Quick Check #89
1. -ive
2. -ial
3. -ive
4. -able
5. -ous
6. -al
7. -al
8. -less
9. -less
10. -able

Quick Check #90
1. perilous
2. commercial
3. heartless
4. laborious
5. natural
6. mysterious
7. predictable
8. believable
9. adventurous
10. medical

Quick Check #91
1. -y
2. -ive
3. -ic
4. -ic
5. -ive
6. -y
7. -y
8. -ent
9. -ic
10. -ent

Quick Check #92
1. masterful
2. basic
3. meaningful
4. attractive
5. different
6. fruity
7. cloudy
8. acidic
9. delightful
10. patient

Quick Check #93
1. -dom
2. -ment
3. -dom
4. -ness
5. -ment
6. -ism
7. -ment
8. -ism
9. -ity
10. -tion

Quick Check #94
1. heroism
2. consideration
3. reality
4. wildness
5. responsibility
6. movement
7. stardom
8. weakness
9. requirement
10. addition

Quick Check #95
1. -ology
2. -ant
3. -ist
4. -ant
5. -or
6. -ery
7. -ist
8. -ery
9. -ology
10. -or

Quick Check #96
1. mythology
2. artist
3. participant
4. painter
5. collector
6. customer
7. server
8. bakery

Quick Check #97
1. -ty
2. -tion
3. -ness
4. -ment
5. -tion
6. -sion
7. -ment
8. -ty
9. -ness
10. -sion

Quick Check #98
1. creation
2. honesty
3. preparation
4. contentment
5. necessity
6. difficulty
7. resentment
8. discussion
9. reaction
10. astonishment

Quick Check #99
1. to break into
2. person who studies Earth
3. study of ancient civilizations
4. measurement of Earth
5. ancient
6. broke out or apart; exploded

Quick Check #100
1. coming from inside of Earth
2. of or relating to the study of ancient civilizations
3. broke; unable to pay debts
4. person who studies ancient civilizations
5. person who studies Earth
6. sudden

Quick Check #101
1. to send out
2. lead
3. by hand
4. to lead in learning or by example
5. act of sending out
6. business related to the field; farming

Quick Check #102
1. person sent to promote a cause
2. farming in the field
3. structure that leads or brings water to a place
4. working by hand
5. a letter or message
6. to lead by convincing

Quick Check #103
1. device that sends written messages
2. created or came up with
3. to send
4. moved
5. sent in for consideration
6. to stop from coming

Quick Check #104
1. came together
2. written signature
3. people who moved to another place
4. allowed to enter or to be sent toward
5. place to come together
6. using written words and images

Quick Check #105
1. large meeting, or a coming together
2. ability to read and write letters
3. able to be heard
4. to build together
5. to see and appreciate
6. showing through pictures

Quick Check #106
1. act of damaging something that was built
2. writing about Earth
3. look at closely
4. building
5. able to be heard; having sound
6. written works

Quick Check #107
1. to listen to
2. able to be seen
3. to change the shape of
4. to go forward; do well in
5. able to be seen
6. a way of showing information

Quick Check #108
1. not able to be seen
2. goes forward
3. follows the shape of
4. went past or beyond
5. relating to sound
6. reshaped

Quick Check #109
1. to build
2. of or related to machines
3. leaning upward
4. something that causes movement
5. bent into angles
6. instrument used to see something small

Quick Check #110
1. piece of machinery
2. framework of something built
3. degrees of bending
4. to lean back
5. instrument used to see something far away
6. further the progress of; move forward

Quick Check #111
1. dome containing life
2. air (around a place)
3. picture (using light)
4. electricity made with water's energy
5. fear of being in closed places
6. using light

Quick Check #112
1. using light for a long distance
2. water structure
3. device used to measure vapor or air
4. fuel made from living matter
5. fear of spiders
6. copy made by using light

Quick Check #113
1. living in the water
2. theater that surrounds a space
3. related to the moon
4. pleasing
5. something against bacteria
6. place where goods are made

Quick Check #114
1. creature able to move on land and in water
2. relating to animals and plants that live near water
3. model; something made to look like
4. thankfulness; state of being pleased
5. related to the moon
6. building where something is made or done

Quick Check #115
1. between planets
2. on top of the ground
3. oversee; watch over
4. asleep
5. below standard
6. between offices or departments

Quick Check #116
1. transportation below the ground
2. tax above regular tax
3. place to sleep
4. eyesight
5. between countries
6. charge above or in addition to regular charge